PEACE
ENDANGERED
The Reality of Détente

On détente:

To make a comparison with chess, this is like two players sitting at a chess board, one of whom has a tremendously high opinion of himself and a rather low opinion of his opponent. He thinks that he will, of course, outplay his opponent. He thinks he is so clever, so calculating, so inventive, that he will certainly win. He sits there, he calculates his moves. With these two knights he will make four forks. He can hardly wait for his opponent to move. He's squirming on his chair out of happiness. He takes off his glasses, wipes them, and puts them back on again. He doesn't even admit the possibility that his opponent may be more clever. He doesn't even see that his pawns are being taken one after the other and that his castle is under threat. It all seems to him like: "Aha, that's what we'll do. We'll set Moscow, Peking, Pyongyang, Hanoi, one against the other." But what a joke! No one will do any such thing. In the meantime, you've been outplayed in West Berlin, you've been very skillfully outplayed in Portugal. In the Near East you're being outplayed. One shouldn't have such a low opinion of one's opponent.

But even if this chess player were able to win the game on the board, carried away by the play, he forgets to raise his eyes; he forgets to look at his opponent and doesn't see that he has the eyes of a killer. And if the opponent cannot win the game on the board, he will take a club from behind his back and shatter the skull of the other chess player, winning the game in that way.

—Aleksandr Solzhenitsyn,
in his speech to the AFL-CIO,
New York, 1975

PEACE
ENDANGERED
The Reality of Détente

by

R. J. RUMMEL

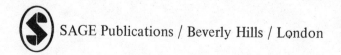 SAGE Publications / Beverly Hills / London

For information address:

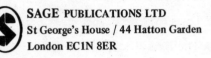

SAGE PUBLICATIONS, INC.
275 South Beverly Drive
Beverly Hills, California 90212

SAGE PUBLICATIONS LTD
St George's House / 44 Hatton Garden
London EC1N 8ER

Printed in the United States of America

Library of Congress Cataloging in Publication Data

Rummel, R.J.

    Peace Endangered.
    1. United States—Defensive. 2. Detente. 3. United States—Foreign relations—Russia. 4. Russia—Foreign relations—United States. 5. Russia—Military policy. I. Title.
UA23.R85   355.03′307′3   76-17372
ISBN 0-8039-0387-1

FIRST PRINTING

Contents

To peace, with freedom and dignity

Preface

The future is purchased by the present.

—Samuel Johnson, *The Rambler*, No. 178

S tudents of international conflict and deterrence have recognized that nuclear stability—the condition of minimal risk of nuclear war—depends on a particular balance of strategic and conventional forces between the major nuclear powers. This balance requires three elements.

First, each side must have a sufficient strategic force to ride out an attack out of the blue and retaliate with unacceptable costs on the attacker's cities. Moreover, neither must develop a first-strike capability—an ability to destroy the other's retaliatory force while keeping in reserve sufficient weapons to threaten its major cities. Such capability will destabilize deterrence by encouraging the other to launch a pre-emptive strike.

Second, each must have military forces that cover the spectrum of possible threats so that neither will take advantage of the weakness in the other's forces, which might motivate the weaker to fall back on its strategic weapons. That is, adequate military power to meet diverse threats discourages recourse to brinkmanship or "massive retaliation."

Third, raising the threshold for the use of nuclear weapons enhances the stability of deterrence. Conventional capability must be able to meet all conventional force threats—such as an attack on South Korea. This is the firebreak theory: once tactical nuclear weapons are used, it is easier to escalate to strategic ones. Avoiding this danger requires conventional forces of sufficient quality and number to handle the threat.

Such is the current theory of deterrence or nuclear peace. Under detente, however, contrary to this theory, we are disarming our conventional forces and seriously deteriorating our nuclear retaliatory capability while increasingly relying on an incredible massive retaliation threat. Moreover, the Soviets simultaneously appear to be going all out for a first-strike capability. In other words, detente is sliding us into a situation in which we will eventually have to choose between nuclear war and strategic surrender to Soviet power.

On what evidence are these conclusions based? Recently I applied the results of comprehensive computer analyses of international behavior, cooperation, and conflict to the assumptions of detente. In addition, I collected military data on the United States and the Soviet Union between 1946 and 1975, and computer-analyzed them to define the trends and military gaps. Finally, I went to mathematical studies of a possible Soviet first-strike capability and of the nuclear offensive power of our Poseidon or future Trident submarine fleet under given conditions.

The results fully substantiated our weakness and the risk of nuclear war: we are now weaker than the Soviet Union; the trends point to even greater weakness; and these trends indicate that the Soviets soon should be able to destroy most of our strategic forces before we are able to retaliate effectively.

Thus this book. Here I shall make clear my own pessimistic

conclusions: Unless we strongly reaffirm our national interest in freedom, recognizing that we are locked into a protracted struggle with totalitarianism, unless we find leaders with the will to persevere and honestly communicate to the American people the profound danger we face, and unless we regain our military superiority, the choice can be only between war or surrender. Soon.

ACKNOWLEDGEMENTS

For access to relevant material, I am indebted to Edward Schwerin, and Chester Ward. Special thanks are owed David Peters for permission to use the University of Hawaii ROTC library; and to Scott Allen for arranging my use of the CINCPAC library.

Special thanks are owed Seungjin Suh for dedicated help in collecting data, Gary Murfin for cheerful aid in running the computer analyses, and Karen Pacheco for typing the manuscript with unexcelled neatness and speed. Scott Allen, Edward Schwerin, and Peter Sybinsky all made helpful comments on portions of the first draft. My wife Grace thoroughly edited the manuscript and deserves credit for whatever clarity this book may have.

The analyses and writing for this book were not done in whole or in part under any government contract or grant.

1979: Again, But...

It is 1979; the battleground, the Middle East. The Egypt-Israel Agreement of September 1, 1975 (Sinai), renewed in 1978, still defines the separation of Egyptian and Israeli forces. Two hundred American civilian technicians monitor troop and aircraft movements at their surveillance stations, and the UN Emergency Force still patrols no man's land between opposing lines. All American efforts for further peace agreements in the Middle East have been fruitless. The month is July.

July 4. Following a series of rapid early morning military movements, explosions rock Cairo, and the world learns that President Sadat has been killed in a pro-Palestinian coup. A "Revolutionary Council" led by popular Air Force General Mobarak has assumed command. In the first formal announcements, the Council proclaims rigid adherence to all treaties and commitments.

July 5-14. The Egyptian Revolutionary Council is strongly in control with wide popular support, as many top officials and officers are purged.

July 14. Syrian President Hafez Assad visits Cairo for talks after which he visits Libya and Algeria.

July 16. King Hussein of Jordan is assassinated, as well-organized and well-armed Palestinian units try to take over control of government buildings in Amman. Fighting breaks out between Palestinians and the Jordanian army.

July 17. With Hussein dead, Jordanian army morale is shaken and fighting is dispirited. Amman is racked by sniper and guerrilla attacks as movement in the capital is brought to a complete halt. Syria proclaims unity with the Palestinian cause and offers aid.

July 18. The Jordanian army declared a truce. Negotiations end with a pro-Palestinian general assuming all power. The Palestinian Republic of Jordan is declared.

July 20. General Mobarak is nominated for President of

Egypt by the National Assembly. A nationwide referendum on the nomination is scheduled for September 2.

August 14-18.

The leaders of Egypt, Jordan, and Syria meet for five days of talks. They announce that all their forces will be put under a unified military command, and that regaining Palestinian territory is the ultimate aim. In a separate statement, Egypt declares that the Sinai Accord is essential to peace in the Middle East. Americans and Israelis are surprised by the moderate tone of the conference.

September 1.

The Organization of Petroleum Exporting Countries (OPEC) meets and Palestinian influence dominates. Along with an expected 12 percent increase in prices, OPEC declares that oil is as important as guns in the final defeat of Israel. Observers see this as a reaffirmation of the threat of an oil boycott in another war with Israel.

September 2.

General Mobarak is elected President of Egypt for a six-year term by 93.2 percent of the votes cast in a national referendum.

September 14.

American reconnaissance satellites show large Egyptian reinforcements being sent across the Nile; significance discounted while UN patrols and American volunteers are in place.

September 15-17.

The Israeli Premier flies to Washington for high-level talks.

September 17.

The American Secretary of State makes a surprise flight to Moscow, ostensibly to discuss a possible breakthrough in the stalled SALT III talks.

September 26.

The Soviet Premier travels to Cairo and Damascus

for three days of talks. The Egyptian War Minister visits Damascus.

September 27. Saudi Arabia declares unity with the Palestinian cause. Two pro-American generals are sacked.

September 28. The American ambassador to Saudi Arabia is recalled for consultation. King Khalid of Saudi Arabia meets with President Mobarak of Egypt.

October 1. Yom Kippur. Specially prepared guerrilla units surround and isolate UN forces and capture American volunteers. United Egyptian, Syrian, and Jordanian forces launch simultaneous attacks across cease-fire lines. The declared aim of this Fifth Arab-Israel War is to recapture lost Arab land and establish a Palestinian state. The Egyptian army rushes two parallel flanking columns through the Gidi and Mitla passes in order to attack significant Israeli air base and logistic center at Refidim. Both columns halted in major air and tank battle. Egypt announces that all American technicians are safe and will be returned immediately to the United States. Washington protests.

October 2. OPEC announces a boycott against all those providing aid to Israel or maintaining diplomatic relations with her. Israel conducts holding actions on Golan Heights and the Jordanian front, and counterattacks against the Egyptian forces. Israel invokes secret clauses of Sinai Accord of 1975 and demands immediate American aid. The UN General Assembly passes a resolution supporting the Palestinian cause.

October 4. Israel launches offensive against Syria. Great Britain and France sever diplomatic relations with Israel.

October 5.   The Soviet Union begins an airlift to Egypt, Syria, and Jordan.

October 7.   Israel stops her Syrian offensive twenty miles from Damascus, while government buildings in Damascus are bombed. OPEC shuts off all oil to the United States.

October 8.   The United States begins to resupply Israel. Japan severs diplomatic relations with Israel.

October 10.   After several days of large tank battles, Israel breaks through and crosses the Nile. Washington freezes the assets of all OPEC nations participating in the U.S. boycott.

October 11-14.   The Soviet Premier visits Cairo.

October 16.   The American Secretary of State again travels to Moscow.

October 18.   Israel now dominates the Sinai and Syria; the Jordanian front is stable. Israel has a large bridgehead on the West Bank, which is rapidly being reinforced. The UN Security Council passes Resolution 397, a joint U.S.-Soviet proposal calling for a cease-fire. Resolution is accepted by Jordan and Egypt, declined by Israel and Syria.

October 19.   Israel completely cuts off the Egyptian Third Army; captures Suez and Ismailia. Cairo lies open to Israel. In an emergency session, the UN Security Council proposes a complete halt to all fighting and a return to the previous cease-fire lines. In a secret message, the United States threatens to cut off aid to Israel unless she accepts the UN resolution.

October 21.   Egypt requests another Security Council meeting
                     and calls for Soviet troops to repel the Israeli
                     invasion. The Soviet Premier sends a message to
                     the American President, demanding Israeli cease-
                     fire and withdrawal, otherwise the Soviet Union
                     will intervene unilaterally. The President places
                     U.S. forces on alert, condition 3.

October 22.   Soviet airlift forces begin mobilizing; her naval
                     units—including a carrier, four missile cruisers,
                     destroyers, and escort ships—move into the eastern
                     Mediterranean. The United States goes on a world-
                     wide advanced readiness alert, condition 2, and via
                     the hotline warns the Soviets against unilateral
                     action, calling for calm discussion and consul-
                     tation. Israeli Hawks are firmly in control and
                     refuse to back down from victory as they did in
                     1973. The U.S. Secretary of State announces a
                     halt to all but medical aid to Israel, and explains at
                     a news conference that this is the only way to get
                     Israel to withdraw and thus reduce the risk of
                     confrontation between the nuclear Powers.

October 23.   Soviet airborne troops land in Egypt. Full military
                     effort is seen. The Soviet Union threatens most
                     serious consequences if the United States inter-
                     venes. The United States intensifies its worldwide
                     alert, condition 1. All nuclear forces are at war
                     readiness, SAC is on airborne alert, and all missile
                     subs, aircraft carriers, and their escorts are
                     deployed at sea. With six hours' advance notice,
                     the President makes a national speech in which he
                     says that the United States cannot allow the
                     U.S.S.R. to intervene unilaterally in the Middle
                     East. It would be inconsistent with agreements
                     governing U.S.-Soviet relations and would give the
                     U.S.S.R. potential control over the oil life blood
                     of Europe and Japan. It would enable her to

exercise decisive political influence over the whole region. Therefore, unless the Soviet Union immediately halts her intervention, the President says, the United States will have no choice but to take counteraction.

October 24.

The first military action between Israeli and Soviet troops occurs on the West Bank. Israel threatens to use all means at her disposal to prevent her destruction, and warns that no state should consider itself invulnerable to attack. Morning Israeli newspapers carry leaks about the possible existence of four 3,700-mile missiles capable of hitting Moscow and of specially prepared, one-way suicide nuclear bombers. Soviet seaborne heavy military equipment is unloaded in Egypt. Soviet General Savkin assumes command of all Egyptian and Soviet forces on the Western front.

Communist demonstrations erupt throughout Western Europe and Britain. Marxist and leftist unions declare national strikes against Zionist and imperialist aggression, and declare fraternal unity with the Palestinian cause. American military movements are hampered; rail and truck routes are sabotaged in West Germany and England. Greece, Italy, and Austria forbid American overflights.

The New York Times headlines "U.S. Backs Down." Reporters trying to uncover why the United States has been so slow to move militarily find insiders giving four reasons: (1) the Soviet Union already has a big foot in the door and has military dominance over the situation; (2) the use of American troops requires extensive consultation with Congress and legislative action, due to the Wadsworth Rider of 1977, requiring consultation with and approval of Congress before any military action is undertaken except in response to an attack on American forces or territory; (3) the lack of European cooperation and anti-American demonstrations and sabotage are preventing military movements; and (4) intervention in the Middle East is a major military effort for which the United States must strip down its NATO forces and continental U.S. reserves. One "unimpeachable source" says that we simply no longer have the power: "Those who have, take." After three days of tumultuous debate, Congress passes a joint resolution giving the President all powers needed to expel the Soviet Union from the Middle East. Polls show 73 percent of the public for American counteraction.

A secret Warsaw Pact meeting and trip to Peking by the Soviet Premier are rumored in Washington. The second day of an extraordinary meeting of the Politbureau is reported.

October 25.

8:00 A.M., Cairo time. General Savkin demands the surrender of all Israeli forces on the west side of the Suez Canal and cessation of all military action in ten hours, or Israeli military and population centers will be attacked. In a coordinated threat, the Soviet Premier declares that four ICBMs now aimed at Israel could completely destroy her forever, and they will be fired if Israel uses any nuclear weapons. Israel begins major evacuations of Tel Aviv, Haifa, and Ramat-Gan, and a partial evacuation of Jerusalem. Through the U.S.-Soviet hotline Israel informs the Soviets that she is capable of attacking Moscow with nuclear weapons, which she will not hesitate to use if her national existence is threatened.

4:00 P.M., Cairo time; 9:00 A.M., Washington time. In a suddenly announced broadcast (simultaneously transmitted in Russian over the hotline), the President of the United States declares that the independence of the Middle East and its oil supplies are essential to the survival of a free

Europe and Japan and absolutely vital to America's security. The independence of the Middle East depends on the Soviet removal of its forces from the region and on the continued national survival of Israel. Therefore, he is calling for the following: (1) immediate cease-fire in place to be monitored by the UN, which has already been accepted by Israel; (2) the subsequent withdrawal of all Soviet forces; (3) the formation of a joint U.S.-U.S.S.R. Peace Commission to establish the boundaries of Israel consistent with the legitimate aspirations of the Palestinians and Israelis for national survival. The U.S.S.R. should have no doubt, the President declares, that a nuclear attack on Israel from any source by any type of missile or bomb will be considered an attack on the United States. Moreover, the United States cannot allow Soviet military forces to remain in the Middle East. The President, declaring this the worst crisis since World War II, invokes his emergency powers.

5:15 P.M., Cairo time. Israel declares a cease-fire in place and agreement with the U.S. peace initiative, but says she will respond to hostile fire.

6:00 P.M., Cairo time. Soviet forces appear to be consolidating and take no action as the ten-hour deadline passes.

7:30 P.M., Moscow time. The Premier accepts a cease-fire and UN intervention, and declares that Zionism and imperialism have been soundly defeated. Moreover, he says that since Soviet troops clearly have achieved their purpose, they will be withdrawn gradually as Egypt is resupplied and Israeli troops are withdrawn as determined by a joint U.S.-U.S.S.R. Commission.

9:00 P.M., New York time. In an emergency session, the UN Security Council passes Resolution 398 calling for a cease-fire and a joint U.S.-U.S.S.R. Peace Commission.

October 27.   The United States stands down from the alert,
                   cancels reserve callup. A *New York Times* headline
                   declares, "U.S. Victory; Crisis Over."

November 2.   4:37 A.M., Washington time; 12:37 A.M. Moscow
                   time. U.S. distant-early-warning line, warning
                   satellites, and space surveillance radar warn of
                   massive Soviet missile launchings. Continental Air
                   Defense Command sets RED alert.
                   4:41. The President is reached and orders an
                   immediate war and nationwide civil-defense alert.
                   Since he has been through many simulations of
                   such radar warning, he follows the long-established
                   contingency plan and therefore withholds firing
                   ICBMs in case of radar misidentification or
                   malfunction.
                   4:47. A message from the Soviet Premier is
                   coming in on the hotline. Highest-priority intelli-
                   gence and State Department communications
                   report full Soviet military mobilization underway.
                   4:48-4:52. All forty-six Strategic Air Command
                   bases are hit by fractional orbital bombardment
                   missile warheads. Most planes are caught on the
                   ground because they had insufficient time to take
                   off in response to alert. Nuclear airbursts are set
                   off over American ICBM fields to create electronic
                   interference with any attempt to launch ICBMs
                   before Soviet silo-destroying warheads arrive.
                   4:50. Still following the established contin-
                   gency plan, the President now refuses to launch
                   missiles in the belief that sufficient silos and
                   missile submarines will survive to be available for
                   post-attack negotiation or selective counterstrikes
                   against military or civilian targets.
                   4:53. Now fully transmitted, the Soviet
                   message to the President recounts American
                   "aggressions" and support of Zionism in the
                   Middle East, and asserts that the U.S.S.R. will not

stand by and allow this to continue. To forestall such aggressive designs, the U.S.S.R. has launched a defensive attack on the homeland of world imperialism. The capitalists should be clear about the following:

> The attack will eliminate most of your long-range bombers and virtually all your ICBMs. A large reserve of our rockets now aimed at 250 of the largest American cities will annihilate them if the United States retaliates against one or more of our cities with its submarine rockets or its surviving bombers or ICBMs. You cannot destroy our reserve rockets; you do not immediately know which have been fired of those in silos, we are capable of reloading many silos already used, and we have hundreds of mobile rockets whose locations are hidden from you. Any rockets launched at military targets in the U.S.S.R. will mean the end of New York. Finally, any attempt at retaliation on our cities will fail. Our SAMs that have been converted to ABMs and our national radar systems now in operation to guide them can destroy your warheads. The worst you can do is cause us several million deaths; in the process you will commit national suicide.

> All we demand is peaceful coexistence. To this end you must destroy your remaining rockets and long-range bombers and permit our inspection teams to verify this. Moreover, your submarines must surface and sail to ports we will designate. Otherwise we will seek them out and eventually destroy them.

> Finally, we demand that you halt all military and economic aid to countries in the

Middle East and immediately cease your imperialist intervention in that region.

You have until 6:00 A.M., Washington time, to accept our demands. After this deadline we will destroy one of your cities for each hour you delay.

5:02-5:07. As the President reads the Soviet message, their ICBM killer warheads explode in airbursts above American silos. Each silo had been targeted with two waves, five minutes apart, of 2-megaton warheads. Forty-seven out of 1,056 silos survive the attack; 4,170,000 Americans die from direct and indirect effects of the destruction of the SAC bases and missile silos; 5 percent of American industrial capacity is destroyed. The United States still remains a viable society, with over 98 percent of its population and 95 percent of its industrial capacity intact, but its deterrence has failed.

5:30. Combined Soviet and Egyptian troops launch a major offensive against Israeli troops.

5:34. The President sends this reply. "We have received your message and warheads. We accede to your demands. You have destroyed our weapons; you have murdered my countrymen. But you have created a hatred in the hearts of all who survive, and a love of freedom which some day will rise to crush you and your system."

5:40. The President informs Israel: "We can no longer help. God be with you."

5:45. The President's national emergency speech is delivered on all radio, television, and military channels:

My fellow Americans, at 5:00 A.M., Washington time, the Soviet Union launched an unprovoked surprise nuclear attack on the United States. This treacherous attack occurred at the very time her diplomats were assuring us of their readiness to negotiate peace in the Middle East.

Millions have died; all our Strategic Air Command bases and virtually all our ICBMs have been demolished. Most of our missile submarines have survived. Our cities were spared.

The Soviet Union has threatened to destroy all our major cities if we retaliate, and to destroy one city for each hour we delay in accepting their demands. Our calculations show that while we cannot seriously damage the Soviet Union, they have the power to devastate our land. Even knowing your rage and desire for swift revenge, as your President I still cannot take those actions which would mean the certain death of most Americans and the tragic destruction of our country.

With no other choice and with the greatest anguish, I have agreed to the following Soviet demands. First, we must scrap all our remaining ICBMs and strategic bombers, and surrender our missile submarines. Second, we must abandon the Middle East.

My countrymen, we have lived through an infamous nuclear attack without firing a shot, but with our nation and society intact. The bitter truth is that the Soviet Union is now the only world Power. We will live in her shadow. The road before us will be cruel, but the spirit of freedom will live, if we so make it. United we will survive. Let us pray. . . ."

November 4.   TASS reports a statement by the Communist Party
                       chief that the heroic armed forces of the Soviet
                       Union have destroyed a single Israeli nuclear
                       bomber fifty kilometers southwest of Kharkov,
                       Ukrainian S.S.R.

The Future as Past

2

What's past is prologue.

—Shakespeare, *The Tempest*, II.i.

The terrifying future projected in Chapter 1 is a somewhat revised chronology of the Yom Kippur War of 1973 with a different finale. I included a likely pro-Palestinian coup in Egypt and the ever-possible assassination of King Hussein of Jordan. But taking into account that in 1979 Yom Kippur will be on October 1, the date and pace of events once the war begins are similar to those of 1973, including the threat of unilateral Soviet intervention, a "savage" message to the President from the Soviet leader, and the American world-wide nuclear alert.

We survived that crisis. Under extreme American pressure. the Israelis agreed to a cease-fire. We were fortunate then, as we were in the Cuban missile crisis of 1962. But as the U.S.S.R. widens her nuclear and conventional superiority, and as Western Europe, the Middle East, or Northeast Asia come under the control of militant leftists or communists, would some future crisis give us no choice but war or surrender?

Consider the scenario again. Most would find it credible up to the November 2 nuclear attack on the United States. Why this attack, when they appeared to have military dominance over the Middle East and were on the edge of complete control over Western oil supplies? The reasoning might be as follows.

Stalin's biggest mistake after 1945 was the Korean War, which caused us to mobilize our resources, more than triple our defense budget, double our armed forces, and build up a military power that the Soviets were wary of for fifteen years. Clearly, Soviet success in the Middle East or a conventional war in the region between the two might again stimulate America to rearm. It might again cause a resurgent fear of communism.

But, within several years the Soviet Union could also have maximum strategic advantage; the United States, becoming alarmed, might undertake initiatives to vastly improve the capability of U.S. strategic forces to withstand a nuclear attack, even considering the automatic launching of American missiles upon satellite warning and radar verification of Soviet missiles heading toward the United States and revising the doctrine of waiting for the Soviets' first blow before taking action.

In any case, in the Soviet view, Israel, supported by Zionist forces in the United States, will never concede. If Soviet forces attack Israel, the United States might retaliate against the U.S.S.R. Although all calculations show that Soviet retaliatory missiles would survive, she must not—as has been her consistent military doctrine—let the capitalists strike the first blow.

Finally, as all Marxist-Leninists recognize, forces are correlated in the communist direction throughout the world and point to a Soviet victory. The Middle East would be the greatest prize; Europe and Japan would then concede Soviet dominance and contribute their vast industrial development to Soviet needs. The good strategist recognizes when he is strongest and his opponent weakest, and when the rewards of striking first are the largest.

Such might be the Soviet arguments. Nonetheless, the surprise use of nuclear weapons still would be incredible to many.

We should always remind ourselves that as it happens and passes into history, a bizarre future becomes understandable, predictable, reasonable. No one believed that Nikita Khrushchev would be "mad enough" to place nuclear missiles in Cuba in 1962. At the time of Nixon's 1972 landslide vote, the story of a Watergate and his resignation would have been a fantasy; in 1962, the story of the fall of Southeast Asia in 1975, absurd; in 1968, a prediction of Nixon's trip to Peking, ludicrous. And, of course, there was the shocking Arab oil boycott and extortion to which the West meekly submitted. Truth is stranger than fiction. *Much of what happens politically in this world would not be accepted as a realistic novel or a probable scenario.*

From our contemporary viewpoint some aspects of the future always will be unthinkable. For this reason a first principle of national security is to hedge one's bets, to think of the worst possible acts of potential enemies and prepare for them, and something more.

But for those who still find the Soviet first use of nuclear weapons farfetched, consider the possible courses events could take as of October 5, 1979, after General Savkin's ultimatum to Israel.

There are three assumptions in the situation that are projections from current trends. First, the United States would be militarily weaker than the U.S.S.R. overall, and particularly in her ability to fight a war in the Middle East. The U.S.S.R. will have the stronger medium-range and tactical air force, army, and navy; she will be better able to move her forces to the region and supply them. Indeed, the analyses shown in this book will indicate that the United States is now generally inferior to the Soviet Union, and that the American trend is downward while the Soviet's is upward.

Second, the Soviets will have already intervened militarily in the Middle East and therefore would have tactical dominance. With the stronger navy in the Mediterranean and nearby air force bases, she could significantly interfere with an American air and sea lift.

Third, the United States would have to strip her continental defense forces and NATO support troops in Europe (in the face of pro-communist demonstrations and sabotage) in order to intervene significantly. This would severely weaken NATO and leave the United States with little reserve to meet a threat or counteraction that the Soviets (or others) could mount elsewhere.

Thus, the United States really has only two alternatives. One is to move to the strategic nuclear level and hope that the threat of nuclear war will cause the U.S.S.R. to back down. In all crises since the Cuban missile crisis of 1962, the Soviets have finally acted prudently and conservatively; therefore American leaders could expect them to so act again. It is the potential contradiction between these American expectations of continued Soviet prudence on the one hand and Soviet perception of American weakness and potential gains on the other that could power an escalation to the nuclear level. This is the scenario presented in Chapter 1.

Or, the United States could concede regional control to the Soviet Union. Without sufficient power to intervene, the United States could diplomatically make the best of a bad defeat and put a UN and peace-making-face on an Israeli surrender and Soviet military occupation of the Middle East. However, in Western Europe, Japan, Africa, or Latin America there would be no doubt that the U.S.S.R. had achieved world dominance, and all had better make the best accommodations possible within the newly forming world communist imperial system.

Between war and surrender. We are approaching this bizarre dilemma with ever-greater speed. The trigger event need not be restricted to the Middle East. It could arise over an anti-communist revolt in East Germany which draws in West Germany; over an invasion of South Korea by the North, involving China and Japan; over a pro-communist revolt in India, in which the U.S.S.R. and China are competitively involved; or over a Soviet attack on China. In any case, we should anticipate that the possibilities include those that, today, we might consider unthinkable. Only the dilemma can be predicted: the choice of either American surrender or nuclear war.

This is the only choice, unless we understand the dilemma and act to avoid it—to prevent increasing Soviet dominance and American weakness.

Kissinger's Equation

3

> Now a common thread runs through all these definitions of détente. They all boil down to the same thing: détente is the avoidance of nuclear war. Détente is the imposition of restraints so that the two super-powers don't blow each other up.
>
> If this is the meaning of détente, then I have a question. What is the difference between détente and cold war? Isn't cold war also an avoidance of hot war?
>
> —George Meany, before the
> Senate Foreign Relations
> Committee, October 1, 1974

Under attack by Senator Henry Jackson and Republican presidential candidate Ronald Reagan, in March, 1976, President Ford dropped détente from his vocabulary in favor of "peace through strength." As a word, détente had become a political liability in his presidential campaign and a cosmetic change was required. The policy, however, remains the same

and it is this policy—which I will continue to call détente—
that concerns me here.

As a policy, then, what is détente? It is a feeling and a
theory; a fear, hope, faith, and belief. It is an equation.

To millions, détente is still a warm word, a good feeling. It
means an end to hostility, a new era of cooperation, a time of
faith, trust, and security. Détente is peace. This impression
has been communicated through numerous speeches by
Nixon, Kissinger, and Ford; through the many documents
and joint principles signed by the United States and the
Soviet Union; through the soothing words of Soviet Communist Party Secretary Brezhnev to the American people.

Because this view has been propagated so successfully,
those who oppose it are ridiculed as Cold Warriors, far
rightists, or congenital anti-communists. Who in his right
mind (read educated, rational, and with humane values)
could speak out against peace—against ending tensions, crises,
and hard feelings?

But his still popular view of détente is not its essence, but
its halo. As an official foreign policy, détente is a process of
relaxing tensions and confrontation—a movement toward
saner relationships. With its emphasis on negotiation, reci-
procity, and mutuality, it is meant to eliminate unilateral
advantage and restrain fishing in troubled waters. The goal is
to minimize conflict and maximize peace.

This process of relaxing tensions does not promise an end
to crises and confrontation, nor an end to political "competition" between the United States and the Soviet Union. Nor,
as so many think, is it an end to the use and importance of
military power. This was stressed in President Ford's American Legion speech in Minneapolis on July 14, 1975, in which
he observed:

> To me détente means a fervent desire for peace—but not peace at
> any price. It means the preservation of fundamental American
> principles, not their sacrifice.

It means maintaining the strength to command respect from our
adversaries and to provide leadership to our friends, not letting
down our guard or dismantling our defenses or neglecting our
allies. It means peaceful rivalry between political and economic
systems, not the curbing of our competitive efforts.[1]

Détente, then, is the relaxation of tensions and confrontation without eliminating competition between the major
powers, or so it would seem. But what drives détente? And
on what theory does it rest?

For an answer, we should examine Secretary Kissinger's
speeches and statements. Before the Senate Committee on
Foreign Relations on September 19, 1974, Kissinger clarified
the principles guiding détente.

The United States cannot base its policy solely on Moscow's good
intentions. But neither can we insist that all forward movement
must await a convergence of American and Soviet purposes. We
seek, regardless of Soviet intentions, to serve peace through a
systematic resistance to pressure and conciliatory responses to
moderate behavior.

We must oppose aggressive actions and irresponsible behavior. But
we must not seek confrontation lightly.

We must maintain a strong national defense while recognizing
that in the nuclear age the relationship between military strength
and politically usable power is the most complex in all history.

Where the age-old antagonism between freedom and tyranny is
concerned, we are not neutral. But other imperatives impose
limits on our ability to produce internal changes in foreign
countries. Consciousness of our limits is recognition of the necessity of peace—not moral callousness. The preservation of human
life and human society are moral values, too.

We must be mature enough to recognize that to be stable a
relationship must provide advantages to both sides and that the
most constructive international relationships are those in which
both parties perceive an element of gain. Moscow will benefit

from certain measures, just as we will from others. The balance cannot be struck on each issue every day, but only over the whole range of relations and over a period of time.[2]

What do these principles mean? Clearly, Kissinger insists on a reliance on military strength, but strength which has a most complex relationship to usable political power. Later in his statement he clarifies his view of military power.

We cannot expect to relax international tensions or achieve a more stable international system should the two strongest nuclear powers conduct an unrestrained strategic arms race. Thus, perhaps the single most important component of our policy toward the Soviet Union is the effort to limit strategic weapons competition.[3]

In other words, there must be a reliance on military strength, but a strength restrained through arms agreements with "our adversaries" based on a *mutual* interest in preventing a nuclear war.

In his principles Kissinger also asserts that we must provide the other side with incentives to maintain the peace. We must create a network of relationships with the Soviet Union so that they have a stake—a vested interest—in relaxing tensions. As he later clarified:

[it] was difficult in the past to speak of a U.S.-Soviet bilateral relationship in any normal sense of the phrase. Trade was negligible. Contacts between various institutions and between the peoples of the two countries were at best sporadic. There were no cooperative efforts in science and technology. Cultural exchange was modest. As a result, there was no tangible inducement toward cooperation and no penalty for aggressive behavior. Today, by joining our efforts even in such seemingly apolitical fields as medical research or environmental protection, we and the Soviets can benefit not only our two peoples but all mankind; in addition, *we generate incentives for restraint.*[4]

Kissinger's equation is clear; he has been consistent in all his public statements about détente. *It is that hostility, tension, overt conflict, and war between adversaries are results of unbridled growth in power and a lack of bonds providing a vested interest in peace. Peace equals controlled power and a web of transactions.* Détente, then, is a fear of nuclear war. Fear is its engine. Détente is also a hope and a belief: hope that power can be restrained, and belief that cooperative transactions lessen conflict. And détente is a faith that arms control and cooperative transactions with the Soviets will buy peace.

The idea of arms control has been a subject of continuing debate and official institutionalization in the Arms Control and Disarmament Agency. As a part of détente, the idea has been transformed into the SALT I agreements with the Soviet Union and the Vladivostok accord signed by President Ford and Secretary Brezhnev.

The belief in "peace through transactions with an adversary" has not been debated. Indeed, it is an untested, unanalyzed assumption lifted from academic social science. This source is betrayed in a speech of Alan Reich, Deputy Assistant Secretary of State for Educational and Cultural Affairs, in which he says:

> When people-to-people bonds and communications networks are more fully developed, there will be a greater readiness to communicate, to seek accommodation, and to negotiate. The likelihood of international confrontation will diminish, and prospects for peaceful solutions will be enhanced. This rationale governs the interest of the State Department in the furtherance of meaningful people-to-people exchange.
>
> In the past few years, social scientists have increasingly studied the relevance of informal nongovernmental communications activities to matters of war and peace. Eminent social scientists such as Dr. Herbert Kelman at Harvard University are attempting to develop a scientific base for these cross-cultural communica-

tions activities. Their research suggests that the existence of informal communications tends to reduce the level of tension when conflicts of interest occur; they contribute to a climate of opinion in which conflicts may be negotiated more effectively. Second, their research indicates that informal relationships create a greater openness in individual attitudes toward other nations, peoples, and cultures; these predispositions also lead to greater readiness to communicate and to resolve differences peaceably. Third, social scientists tell us that international cooperation and exchange contribute to world-mindedness and to an internationalist or global perspective on what otherwise might be viewed either as purely national or essentially alien problems. Finally, international people-to-people relationships help develop enduring networks of communication which cut across the likelihood of polarization along political or nationalist lines.[5]

This belief has gained adherents among academic scholars of international relations, and there is voluminous literature which asserts that transactions bind nations together and promote peace. As a former teacher of international relations Secretary Kissinger is no doubt familiar with this literature, and perhaps its influence on him can be seen through détente.

At its roots, therefore, détente is the equation that peace equals arms control—restraint on power—and cooperative transactions. As I will show later, when subjected to computer analysis this equation simply does not hold. Indeed, the computer reveals in detail that arms control has caused a unilateral American reduction while the Soviet Union has driven toward a massive military buildup, quite contrary to détente. Moreover, it proves that cooperative transactions do not generally lead to peace. In fact, cooperative transactions for the Soviet Union and China have as often, if not more often, led to conflict.

But before presenting these results, some discussion of the nature of conflict, power, and international relations will provide a context for understanding the fallacy of Kissinger's equation and the meaning of the computer results to be presented.

NOTES

1. *The New York Times,* August 20, 1975, p. 12.
2. *The Department of State Bulletin,* Vol. LXXI (October 14, 1974).
3. Ibid., p. 512.
4. Ibid., p. 510, italics added.
5. "People-to-People Diplomacy—Key to World Understanding," *The Department of State Bulletin,* Vol. LXVII (September 4, 1972).

Does Cooperation Buy Peace?

> *Leonid I. Brezhnev, the Soviet Communist party leader, has emphasized to Eastern European leaders that the movement toward improving relations with the West is a tactical policy change to permit the Soviet bloc to establish its superiority in the next 12 to 15 years.*
>
> *—International Herald Tribune,*
> September 18, 1973, p. 2

Peace is secured by cooperative transactions, or so Kissinger believes. To deal with this equation, let me break it into two parts. The first is the belief that the more transactions there are between two nations, the more harmony or less conflict there will be in their relations. This I call Détente I, and I will analyze it in this chapter and present salient computer results in the next. The second part—Détente II—is the hope that by restraining power there will be less conflict; I will consider this systematically in subsequent chapters.

Trade promotes harmony. Person-to-person contact provides goodwill. State visits and international conferences advance understanding. And treaties and international organizations institutionalize peace. These beliefs are deeply and widely held, both among fervent idealists and seasoned diplomats and statesmen. Détente I is simply one of its current manifestations.

If we understand international cooperation to comprise a range of collaborative activities between nations, such as exports, treaties, governmental and nongovernmental international organizations, international conferences, tourists, student exchanges, and the like, then this belief can be summarized thus: *cooperation and conflict are opposites.* International cooperation negates conflict. Cooperation drives conflict away by deflating the potentiality for violence and war always inherent in man's social relationships.

In other words, cooperation and conflict between nations form a single dimension. Like hot and cold, soft and hard, or love and hate, they cannot coexist in the relations between two nations. To move toward cooperation is to move away from conflict; to emphasize confrontation is to turn away from collaboration.

This belief is wrong, sociologically and politically. Cooperation and conflict are not opposites, but complements—they are intrinsic parts of the social process among nations. They are separate dimensions reflecting phases in the process of building a mutual society, a structure of common norms, expectations, and laws.

Nations are diverse in culture and societies. Each has its own systems of meanings, values, and norms, its own religions, ethics, laws, arts, philosophies, and sciences. Each is governed by differing ideologies and political systems. Finally, each is a complex of different institutional powers (such as government bureaucracies, the military services, and legislatures), associational interests (such as businesses and professional groups), and communal groups (such as the church and racial-ethnic groups). No nation speaks only one tongue; and the tongues it does speak are often incomprehensible, because they grow out of cultural meanings and assumptions unknown in other nations.

Thus, each nation is a unique sociocultural specimen. It stands alone. Only its members can truly understand a culture's perspective, personality, desires, and goals. In this sense all mankind is not one, not an indivisible whole. Internationally speaking, mankind is a collection of variegated cultures, each comprising the sole universe of meaning to its members.

The profound international question, then, is: if all national cultures such as the Indonesian, Brazilian, Chinese, Swiss, Russian American, and so on are diverse universes, *how do cultures establish and maintain working relationships among themselves?* How is cooperation established and enhanced? How do different nations cross the incommensurable divide among them to communicate and cooperate?

To a contemporary international businessman, scholar, or diplomat, this question may seem curious. Businessmen, for example, establish contacts with their foreign counterparts to negotiate the conditions of trade. Interpreters are employed, and cultural go-betweens may smooth over differences as terms of trade or investment are negotiated. The bargaining may be hard and cultural differences may cause some misunderstanding, but deals are struck. It "ain't no big thing"—nothing like that implied by the abstract notion of cultures as separate universes.

To the scholar or government official who attends an international conference, the differences among cultures is patent, unarguable. But at the conference different nationalities reach out to communicate and share ideas, and often common position papers and recommendations emerge. Again, diverse cultures can cooperate.

The problem with such perceptions is that, as with other activities, international business and conferences are conducted within an established framework. Norms have been determined for governing the relationship, expectations have developed through previous interaction, and an overall political framework sets the limits. In other words, such transactions occur within an international, regional, or bilateral order—a *structure of expectations*—that bridges the gap among diverse cultures. The question, then, is not how cultures can establish relations within an existing framework, but how is the framework itself formed?

Consider this example. A Russian and an American are marooned on a small deserted island. Socioculturally, they have in common only similar circumstances (although no doubt differently perceived) and the basic human need for food, sleep, security, self-assertion, and self-esteem. Each is a separate universe, an individual psyche and cultural reality. How do they establish some common framework which enables each to satisfy both his own interests and their common needs? The answer is through a process of interaction that has elements of order and disorder, harmony and opposition, cooperation and conflict.

This process is a unity, an integrated movement in the interaction of individuals. But to comprehend and relate this two-person process to international relations, let us refract the process through a prism and view its elementary colors. The first is *interests*. Each individual has interests—that is, active goals he wants to achieve. These are linked to his needs, which provide psychic energy for working toward their gratification. In content, interests have meaning and complexity derived from a person's culture and experience. The interest in putting a double lock on one's front door or reducing the risk of nuclear war, as in détente, are specific in meaning to society and culture, but they both relate to a common need for security. Interests, therefore, are the basic manifestations of sociocultural differences at the individual level.

The second element is *capability*. The capabilities of a person are his basic powers such as intelligence, memory, strength, speed, and so on. Capability is often called power, of which military strength at the international level is a particular kind.

The third element is *credibility*. A person's credibility is a two-sided concept, depending on whether we are viewing him from within or without. From within, credibility means a person's *will* to follow through on his promises or threats to others; from without, credibility is the *faith* one can have in another's promises or threats. Our daily lives are a complex net of relations with others based on credibility. When we order food in a restaurant, we believe the owner's menu to be credible in its assertions; the owner believes us to be credible paying customers. Our children develop a faith in our promises and a respect for our threats, and this helps order the family. And when we establish relations with people for the first time, we are concerned to demonstrate credibility in numerous small ways.

Interests, capability, and credibility are the major elements of social interaction. Interests comprise goals and the strength of motivation to achieve them; capabilities are the means of gratifying interests; and credibility is a person's will to use capability to satisfy interests and others' perception of this will.

Now, to return to our Russian and American castaways. Each has interests and capabilities, but these are unknown to each other. How do they reach across the void that separates them? They meet, perhaps by accident, are surprised, and try to communicate. Gestures, pictures in the sand, simple sounds are their first media. They know each other to be human, and thus have prior expectations about their mutual need for food and sleep, about their mutual ability to communicate, and about their mutual potentiality for cooperation or violence.

Out of their initial attempts, they will establish some balance between their interests of the moment, their perceived capabilities (one may be a much larger man, the other may have a knife), and their credibilities. This is a *balance* of interests, capabilities, and credibilities, of goals, power, and will. This balance forms a common structure of expectations, an initial structure of understandings, expectations, a division of labor, and a status quo; a structure informally defining who gets what, when, and how.

But such an initial structure of expectations can only imperfectly reflect the underlying reality. Nonetheless, it serves as a first framework for cooperative interaction between the two. This interaction, in turn, brings greater familiarity as different interests emerge and capabilities are recognized. With further interaction, however, such as jointly hunting for water or building a shelter, the initial structure of expectations becomes increasingly incongruent with the emerging interests. The first balance becomes unsuitable, and there is an effort toward replacing it with one more in tune with changing interests, credibilities, and capabilities.

Then, usually, some event will trigger the disruption of the initial structure of expectation. Some final straw such as one's perception of the other working less than he should or an unexpected event like a storm may cause a dispute, an argument, a fight. This *conflict* will then serve as a mechanism for the rebalancing of interests, capabilities, and credibilities. It will produce a more realistic mutual perception and division of rights and duties. Conflict will transform the initial structure of expectations into a new and more valid order.

To conclude this extended metaphor, the castaways are two quite separate sociocultural and psychological universes who build a bridge across which they can communicate and cooperate through tentative structures of expectation. *Each structure is a framework of order, a status quo.* But change is a constant of life, and people learn from their cooperative interactions. Each structure is temporary, a momentary balance among the ever-changing perceived interests, capabilities, and credibilities of participants. *And conflict, then, is both the signal that a structure has been disrupted and the means for building a more compatible balance.*

What does this simplified metaphor say about diverse national cultures and ideologies in contact, such as the American and Soviet? The metaphor is more precise than it may seem at first. We are all stranded on a planet with limited resources and finite territory. We are all establishing mutual frameworks of order within which we can cooperate, or we are already transacting within a pre-established structure of expectations. And underlying all these orders is a balance of national and cultural interests, of capabilities (power), or credibilities. Finally, conflict and violence among cultures indicates a breakdown in a division of labor, rights, norms, and understandings.

The many conflicts that occur among nations, therefore, should be viewed as neither pathological nor the antitheses of cooperation. International conflict is an intrinsic aspect of change—the means of rebalancing between cultures, the engine of cooperation. Conflict and cooperation are parts of the same international social process moving through time: order, disorder, order; balance, rebalancing, balance; structure of expectations, conflict, structure of expectations.

Of course, nations interact within many structures of expectations. There are global structures of the major world powers, the United Nations, and international organizations;

regional ones such as NATO, the Common Market, and ASEAN; and bilateral ones, such as the SALT I treaty between the United States and the Soviet Union. These structures cover different functional areas, such as terms of trade, the .international economic system, military balances, immigration, and tourism. Frequently some are disrupted and re-formed through conflict, independently of others that exist between nations, but seldom are all structures involved simultaneously. When they are, the conflicts are most violent.

Thus, between any two cultures we would expect multiple structures of expectations governing cooperation which are in various states of incongruence with underlying interests, capabilities, and credibilities.

Moreover, we would expect overt conflict between two nations to be *independent* of any one structure because conflict depends upon some trigger event that causes nations to rebalance an incongruent structure of expectations, and the timing of such a trigger event is unpredictable. Second, conflict between cultures in the aggregate is a composite of conflict behaviors associated with many different kinds of balancing. This aggregate, therefore, will be independent of any one structure, although we know that a specific conflict will be connected to the disruption and rebuilding of a specific structure of expectations.

The answer to the question, then, as to whether cooperation buys peace and harmony between nations is this: *Cooperative transactions may increase or decrease conflict and tension.* Cooperation must be in line with the interests, credibility, and capabilities of the nations involved. Otherwise, conflict will occur. Moreover, rather than disrupting cooperation, conflict may be the means to balance interests, credibility, and capability of the adversaries to enhance harmonious relations.

Conflict and cooperation are part of a social process of bridge building between separate cultural and political universes. They are therefore related aspects of reaching out and establishing international communication and trans-actions. Conflict and cooperation are not opposites; they are *complements*. They are not the opposite ends of a single dimension, but are two dimensions (facets) of the social process. The opposite of cooperation is a total lack of com-munication or collaboration; the opposite of conflict is the absence of conflict.

Such is the relationship between cooperation and conflict, for men cast away on a deserted island, strangers establishing social relations, newly married couples, or interacting nations. The next chapter will add more detail to this picture for international relations.

The Reality of Détente I

5

As theory, Détente I is false—cooperative transactions do not necessarily buy peace; cooperation and conflict are not opposites, but complements. What do we find when we examine the way nations actually behave? When all the data we can possibly collect are analyzed through the computer, do the results support Détente I? An answer requires some preliminary discussion of the data and the nature of the findings.

Rocket into space for a moment for an astronaut's view of planet Earth. Each nation is colored differently and the interactions among them—exports, tourists, state visits, treaties, migration, joining international organizations, forming alignments, making threats and diplomatic protests, and so on—are seen as light tracks on an oscilloscope. Clearly, for pairs of nations with dense interactions such as Japan and the United States, the lights would coalesce into a wide beam; for others such as South Korea and Afghanistan, there would be only a few distinct light tracks. For some, such as Iceland and Outer Mongolia, there may be no track at all. When these movements of light *illuminate cooperative activities,* and form distinctly separate patterns of tracks and beams moving in different directions, *we have distinctly different structures of expectations between nations.*

The actual cooperative behavior among nations reflects their underlying expectations. Where these behaviors form different patterns, we have different structures of expectations—that is, distinct balances of interests, capabilities, and credibilities. Like a flock of birds flying together in the same direction, cooperative transactions move and change direction simultaneously, forming a common pattern—a visual pattern—quite distinct from others flying about. Birds can fly and maneuver in such a close formation because they have developed a common structure of expectations.

The question, then, is what separate structures of expectations do we find among nations? Hundreds of computer analyses of thousands of international interactions have been done to define these patterns. The technical details and data are given elsewhere,[1] and are not of concern here. The general computer results for all the conflictful and cooperative bilateral interactions among Brazil, Burma, China, Cuba, Egypt, India, Indonesia, Israel, Jordan, the Netherlands, Poland, the United Kingdom, the Soviet Union, and the

United States for the years 1950, 1955, 1960, 1963, and 1965 are as follows.

The largest pattern of interaction between two nations includes a diversity of *transactions,* such as the export of books, comembership in intergovernmental and nonintergovernmental international organizations, conferences, total exports, and tourists. This is not simply a trade pattern, for the involvement of tourists, international organizations, and books shows that two nations displaying this pattern have a social and cultural salience transcending the contractual exchange of goods.

This pattern also reflects a common structure of expectations. It indicates that a system of understandings, agreements, and norms knit together these diverse interactions, so that an increase in one transaction tends to be followed by an increase in another.

In the overall interactions between nations, however, there is another, quite distinct, pattern of transactions. This consists of the flow of students between two nations, state visits, treaties entered into, and proportion of exports, with student movement being the core of the pattern. Here a structure of expectations is centered on *student* exchange, but also involves a certain formalization through treaties and high-level discussions.

A third pattern of interactions is purely organizational and formal, involving comemberships in intergovernmental and nonintergovernmental organizations alone, whether as a simple count of the number of such comemberships or taking into account the size or the importance to members of these organizations. This *international organization* pattern represents a formal-legal structure of expectations among nations, one that is quite apart from the two transaction patterns.

According to much that is written about international affairs, nations only trade or fight. The above patterns contradict this. But we do find a separate and distinguishable *trade* pattern made up of the relative exports of one nation to another. Exports, whether as a proportion of Gross National Product (GNP) or of total exports manifest their own direction and pattern—structure of expectations. Thus, the activities of business or government in negotiating and trading goods is separate from those expectations involved in joining international organizations, the movements of students, or other transactions between nations.

The above structures underlie what might be called "functional international relations." They comprise understandings and norms guiding the interactions between citizens or governments in terms of their private interests and socioeconomic needs.

In summary, we find four major cooperative patterns, each actualizing a separate set of understandings between nations. They are manifested as transactions, student flows, international organizations, and relative exports, and we find *not one correlated with conflict behavior, either positively or negatively.* This scientific finding is consistent across many studies.

Instead, we discover that conflict behavior forms four separate patterns. One is a pattern of military defense alignments and voting conflict over UN issues. Nations which are not aligned militarily tend to oppose each other in UN voting. This is surely a *political conflict* or alignment pattern. A second pattern, of *negative behavior,* comprises public accusations, diplomatic protests, negative sanctions (such as boycotts or embargoes), and expelling or recalling ambassadors. A third independent conflict pattern is that of *military action,* specifically warning and defensive acts (alerts, mobilizations, cancellations of leaves, troops or naval movements, etc.) and the fact and intensity of military actions. Finally, a fourth consists of the all too familiar *anti-foreign demonstrations*, such as attacks on embassies and foreign nationals or their property.

Thus, overall interactions between nations fall into separate cooperative and conflictful patterns. But to be sure that these are *independent* patterns, we must take one more look at the range of interactions. The patterns themselves may be correlated. For example, traffic patterns are correlated with weather patterns, and distinct authoritarian and totalitarian patterns of government are correlated (both have a number of features in common).

Additional computer analyses of the eight international patterns indicate that a number of them are correlated and combine into a more general cluster of activities. Specifically, we have uncovered a higher-order cooperative pattern comprising correlated transaction, student, international-organization, and export subpatterns. This means that a general cooperative structure of expectations integrates the separate patterns we originally found. Cooperation thus occurs at two levels: it manifests a particular system of understandings and norms, a specific balance of interests, capabilities, and credibilities; and these specific balances occur in a larger order, a general cooperative framework which provides direction and guidance to all these activities.

However, we also find two general, higher-order patterns completely uncorrelated with cooperation. One is a general combination of the two original patterns of political conflict and negative behavior, and the other is of military action and anti-foreign demonstrations. In other words, conflict forms completely independent higher-order patterns of behavior between two nations.

However, all the computer results summarized so far have been of the interactions among a variety of nations, including India, Brazil, the Netherlands, and so on. It may well be that the interactions of the big powers are different by virtue of their world interests and responsibilities. Let us descend from our global perspective and focus on the full range of cooperative and conflictful bilateral interactions of China, the Soviet Union, and the United States with all other nations.

A computer analysis of 7,296 cases of bilateral interaction for China with as many as 112 other nations for the years 1950, 1955, 1960, 1963, and 1965 showed conflict and cooperative interaction to be uncorrelated.[2] Similar analyses of 4,592 cases of bilateral interaction of the Soviet Union with 82 nations for 1960 and 1965 also showed conflict and cooperation were uncorrelated.[3] Finally, analyses of 1,539 cases of bilateral American interactions with 81 nations for 1955,[4] 4,592 cases of interactions with 82 nations for 1960 and 1965,[5] and 1,908 cases of bilateral interactions with 106 nations in 1963[6] showed clearly that cooperation and conflictful behavior were uncorrelated.

The undeniable conclusion is that a knowledge of the level and nature of the cooperative transactions between a major power and another nation does not enable one to predict or forecast the level and nature of conflict. This not only holds true for the communist powers, but for America as well.

Conflict and cooperation *are* empirically independent. They form separate dimensions. They are not opposites, but complementaries. Such is suggested by a firm grasp of sociopolitical fundamentals; such is supported by scientific analyses of actual interactions. Theoretically *and* empirically, Détente I is false. Cooperative transactions do not buy peace. Not for the Soviet Union or China, or even for America.

NOTES

1. R. J. Rummel, *Applied Factor Analysis* (Evanston: Northwestern University Press, 1970); *Dimensions of Nations* (Beverly Hills: Sage,

1972); *National Attributes and Behavior* (Beverly Hills: Sage, in press, 1976).

2. R. J. Rummel, *Field Theory Evolving* (Beverly Hills: Sage, in press), Chapter 13.
   3. Ibid., Chapter 14.
   4. Ibid., Chapter 10.
   5. Ibid., Chapter 14.
   6. Ibid., Chapter 11.

Does Restraining Power Buy Peace?

After the [June, 1967] war, the Soviet Union helped Egypt and Syria recover their military and economic power. In the last few years it has helped in every possible way to tip the balance of power in favor of the Arabs. Without this, it would have been impossible for Egypt and Syria to score their successes of the last war of October 1973 in the Middle East.

—Radio Moscow, April 4, 1974

In Chapter 4, I provided a foundation for understanding the basic relationship between cooperative transactions and conflict. That is, cooperation occurs within a structure of expectations based on a mutual balance among the interests, credibilities, and capabilities of the participants. If the structure and these underlying elements become unbalanced, tension is produced, a disruption of the structure becomes increasingly likely, and eventually some trigger will provoke conflict. This conflict will produce a new status quo and interactions more in line with changed interests, credibilities, and capabilities.

This understanding is also basic to comprehending the role of power in international conflict.

Power comes in many forms. There is the power of love and the power of intellect. The power of coercion and of authority. To focus just on coercive power—that is, on a nation's military strength—is to overlook the variety of ways in which power is packaged.

In particular, three kinds of power largely order international relations and support peace. One power comprises the direction and strength of *national interests*. A deeply felt interest will provide the nation with an assertiveness and potency in international relations far surpassing its military strength. Such has been Israel's power, and North Vietnam's. The lack of such interests is now America's weakness.

Along with national interests there must be a will to defend and assert these interests. Power also involves the will to fight and win, to uphold fundamental values, and to follow through on commitments. Will is a nation's power to act.

From the perspective of other nations, will power is a nation's credibility. It is the degree to which a nation will stand behind its threats or honor its commitments.

America lacked the will to fulfill its commitments to South Vietnam. This demonstrated lack of credibility has had severe repercussions on such American allies as South Korea, the Philippines, Thailand, and Japan, and the United States has lost much of its influence with these countries as a consequence. This is a loss of power, of the ability to control events.

Finally, there is capability, or military strength. The role of such power need not be labored here. No one doubts that it is an aspect of power; indeed, it is often mistaken for power's essence.

Power is then made up of interests, credibility, and military capability. If any of these elements is zero, then a nation effectively has no power. Without interest or will, no matter how much military power a nation has, it will be defeated by a militarily weaker nation. The United States had the military power to annihilate North Vietnam, but lack of interests and will led to our subsequent defeat. Similarly, the Arabs have always had the military power to defeat Israel; they simply have not had Israel's strong interests and will.

However, even if a nation has strong interests and will power to match, it can do little without military capability.

Thus, interests, credibility, and capability form a triangle of power. When we speak of a balance of power in international relations, it is of a mutual balance among these three elements. And it is this balance that undergirds the cooperative relations between nations.

If any element changes—if interests flag, if credibility comes into question, if capability shifts—the structure of expectations guiding international relations becomes ripe for disruption. Conflict is then likely, and all it needs is some trigger.

Détente II—the emphasis in detente on restraining military capability—considers neither interests nor credibility, but focuses on military strength as the variable most related to conflict. Its principle is that arms control will lessen conflict. And in this Détente II ignores the following.

Restraining military power has undermined American credibility. The loss of South Vietnam, Cambodia, Laos and Angola; our removal of military bases overseas and the withdrawal of American troops, such as a division from South Korea; the SALT I accords, which have given the Soviet Union a clear military advantage in many strategic areas; and our refusal to compete with the Soviets' remarkable across-the-board drive for military superiority are hardly evidence of America's will and interest in fighting aggression and subversion.

Restraining military power has eroded American interests. America's clear interest was, at one time, to help those anywhere who were fighting for freedom against aggression or subversion and to contain communism. These goals, which helped limit the growth of communism and provided strength to American foreign policy, are now muddied and confused. Influenced by the halo of détente, the glowing descriptions of our various arms-control agreements with the U.S.S.R., and Soviet lip service to the end of the Cold War, many see America's primary interests to be domestic, environmental, or Third World matters. No longer is freedom the banner or resisting communism the battle cry; ameliorating poverty, preserving resources, and disarmament are now fashionable.

Thus in the *belief* that restraining military power will reduce conflict American power *has been* so restrained. And this while the Soviet Union's superordinate interest in defeating the West is as strong as it ever was and the Soviets' credibility around the world has been maintained by their invasion of Czechoslovakia, their massive aid to North Vietnam, their strong support of the Arabs in the 1973 Middle East war, and their decisive aid to the victorious Marxist faction in Angola.

The consequence is then a dangerous shift in the balance of power toward the U.S.S.R. This balance was painfully developed throughout the Cold War and as a result of numerous crises, such as the Berlin Blockade of 1948, the Suez crisis of 1956, the Berlin crises of 1958 and 1961, the Cuban missile crisis of 1962. This balance—the foundation of the structure of expectations between the two nuclear powers—is no longer stable. But the structure of expectations remains the same: The same status quo is locked in place for the two nations. The international order in terms of what belongs to whom is largely the same as it was during the Cold War, with the important exception of Southeast Asia.

With a U.S.-U.S.S.R. status quo largely unaltered and a shift in the balance of power toward the revolutionary powers, it is only a matter of time before some trigger event disrupts the structure—perhaps another war in the Middle East, as outlined in Chapter 1.

It is clear that a focus on restraining military strength to lessen conflict is a grievous error. A singular concern with capabilities without considering the impact on one's interests and credibilities, in fact, can lead to a perilous shift in the balance of power and increase the likelihood of conflict.

An analysis of the fundamentals shows that Détente II is also false. But what about the actual behavior of nations? Does their behavior in relation to their capabilities lend substance to Détente II? This is the subject of the next chapter.

The Reality of Détente II

> *I cannot understand the argument that we should reduce our military strength as a contribution to the national search for peace. In my experience, military strength is not an alternative to a national search for peace. It is an essential element of it. In the world as it is, and is likely to be for the indefinite future, military strength and diplomacy are fingers of the same hand. A national commitment to the search for peace not backed up by military strength would not be a policy at all. It would be a pious expression of hope, devoid either of credibility or effect.*
>
> —Alexis U. Johnson,
> *The Department of State Bulletin,* Vol. LXVII
> (September 11, 1972)

If there is some substance to Détente II—the belief that restraining military capabilities secures peace—it should be reflected in the world as it is. The first problem is to measure adequately military capability among nations and then relate it to their conflict.

Over several years I have carried out numerous computer analyses of data on hundreds of national characteristics of nations to determine the dimensions of nations. Most of the results have been published.[1] A consistent finding was a capabilities dimension which closely approximates military power. This dimension involves the size of the armed forces of a nation, its defense budget, its area and population, national income, and its energy production times its population. Thus, military power is measured in terms not only of raw strength but also of a nation's space, people, income, and energy. I will refer to this as a *military capability dimension.*

The question is: Among the many dimensions of nations, such as level of development, type of political system, culture, size, and military capability, what most relates to conflict and peace? As one would expect, the computer analyses of about 70,000 pieces of information on attributes and behavior for all nations between 1950 and 1965 showed that the total foreign conflict of a nation is most positively related to military capability. That is, the greater the capability of a nation, the more its total conflict.

However, Détente II concerns not so much the total conflict of the United States, but of U.S.-U.S.S.R. conflict. Therefore, bilateral relations are of greatest concern.

Several dozen computer analyses were done bearing on the relationship of military capability to bilateral relations and conflict. Differences in the military capability of nations along with their differences in development, political systems, and culture were systematically related to their cooperative transactions and their conflict.[2]

The results show that military capability again is the significant dimension. Nations tend to direct their bilateral conflict behavior toward those whose military capability is clearly superior within the international system, so that the most militarily powerful nation tends to have the most conflict behavior directed toward it.

However, for any two nations that are selected randomly, knowing simply whether they are or are not equal in military capability does not allow us to predict their conflict behavior. Even in bilateral relations it is a nation's military status among *all* nations that counts.

Thus, military capability is significant only for gauging the level of conflict within the entire system of nations. This is not to deny the dimension's salience in bilateral relations, but there is no constant relationship between a particular kind of difference in capability and conflict. Neither military parity nor superiority *by itself* lessens conflict; only extreme military weakness will.

How do we interpret these results? They are consistent with the influence of capability on peace in terms of its triangular relationship to interests and credibility. Recall that conflict is a result of a changing balance among these three elements and only these three. Therefore, the relative development of nations, their differing political systems, or their unique cultures should not, by themselves, show much relationship to conflict and peace. *This is what, in fact, I found.*

Moreover, since only the three elements should be related to conflict, then military capability, as one of them, should have such a relationship. *This also is a result.*

Now, I also found that neither parity nor superiority in military capability is associated with bilateral peace. The reason is that capability, by itself, does not bring peace unless there is no capability at all; it is the balance among interests, credibilities, *and* capability that brings peace.

It is dominance in *political* power that deters conflict and war—where political power equals vital interests, the will to pursue these interests, and the strength (capability) to do so.

With regard to Détente II, I can say the following based on the preceding chapter and these computer results. The emphasis on military capability in its relation to conflict is correct. However, military capability alone is insufficient to affect the bilateral conflict and violence between the Soviet Union and the United States unless we disarm altogether. The fallacy in Détente II is not the emphasis on military capability as a crucial variable, but in the belief that restraining capability and maintaining parity (or "essential equivalence") will improve the chances for peace.

Peace results from political dominance—*a dominance not alone in military capability, but also in the strength of a nation's interests and the force of its will.* It was through this kind of dominance that America maintained the peace throughout the Cold War years against the most aggressive and imperialist revolutionary power since Napoleon's France. Restraint of American military capability and elaboration of the virtues and peaceful consequences of détente have devitalized the interests and crippled the will which have sustained the peace. The balance of power thereby has been seriously altered, and *as a result war is more likely, not less.*

These analyses aside, there are other beliefs about Détente II and conflict, especially bearing on the risks of nuclear war, that must be considered. One is that the restraint in American armaments has not produced a situation of Soviet superiority, and that we remain militarily superior. Is this indeed the case? Second is the belief that the United States and the Soviet Union have been engaged in an action-reaction arms race. Someone, so it is felt, must take the first step to halt the arms race, for if this cycle is not broken, greater tension and a greater risk of nuclear war are inevitable. But has there been an arms race? And has the U.S.S.R. been responsive to quantitative and qualitative changes in our armaments? I shall deal with these questions in the following chapters.

NOTES

1. R. J. Rummel, *Dimensions of Nations* (Beverly Hills: Sage, 1972), and *National Attributes and Behavior* (Beverly Hills: Sage, in press, 1976).

2. Ibid.; also, R. J. Rummel, *Field Theory Evolving* (Beverly Hills: Sage, in press).

The Myth of American Military Superiority

8

Q: Wasn't détente supposed to be a "live and let live" arrangement that would avoid more military build-ups?

A: The Soviets do not use the term "detente." They use the term "peaceful coexistence," which is a phrase coined by Lenin and employed by Stalin. The Soviets see détente as a way to avoid the risk of war and expand their power relative to their former opponents.

James R. Schlesinger, interview in
U.S. News & World Report
May 26, 1975

. . . the sheer massiveness of Soviet strategic nuclear programs is staggering.

—General George S. Brown, Chairman,
Joint Chiefs of Staff, at
Armed Forces Staff College,
January, 1975

Détente's basic goal is to reduce the risk of nuclear war by imbedding our adversary in a web of transactions and cooperative arrangements (Détente I) while maintaining, but restraining, our military power (Détente II). Nixon, Kissinger, and now Ford all have been very clear: Détente II does not mean American inferiority. It does mean reducing the tensions that lead to war, and one source of tension is an arms race. Thus unilateral restraint, and thus the SALT I ABM treaty and the Vladivostok Accords limiting warheads.

That Détente II has not weakened the United States has been reiterated by Secretary Kissinger.

I have always believed that I would not exchange our strategic forces for the Soviet forces. We are ahead in every significant category.[1]

Basically, I do not agree with those who say the balance of power is shifting against us. I think we ought to distinguish between briefings that are given in which naturally those who want more appropriations are stating the worst possible thing that can happen, from how the situation may look to the other side.[2]

But it must be understood that Kissinger is talking not about a decisive military advantage but of an "equivalence of forces" in which the United States has maintained the edge.

An essential question, then, is whether Détente II does in fact describe the military balance. Or do the words of Détente II cloak a real American military inferiority?

Figure 8.1 describes the current military balance. The center vertical line is military parity. The length of the bar to the right or to the left measures the percentage superiority of the U.S.S.R. or the United States over the other.[3] To make sure the chart is clear, consider the total armed forces classified under general indicators. The chart shows that in 1975 the Soviets' armed forces were 109 percent greater than ours.

Down the left side of the chart are listed all the indicators of the military balance for which, as of April, 1976, I could find current data. I have listed in Appendix B the major data sources used to collect these data and those used in the subsequent chapters.

A word on the quality of the data before continuing. Data in public sources on American and Soviet military capabilities vary widely depending on which sources and definitions of weapons (e.g., what is a cruiser) are used. They are subject to political manipulation or may be mere educated guesses. Nonetheless, it is possible to get approximate figures and to discern the profile of military power in spite of these difficulties. My sense for the data and my discussions with those privy to classified data strongly suggest that the profile of the military balance shown in the chart reflects reality.

With the figure as a background let us now examine the military balance in detail.

GENERAL INDICATORS

The general indicators show the overall balance regarding those aspects cutting across many military functional divisions, such as the army and navy. On all these general indicators, the Soviets surpass us by large, dangerous margins which are rapidly growing as they build up and we disarm.

From 1968 to 1975 (the era of détente), the American *armed forces* were demobilized by 40 percent to 2.1 million men, while the Soviets increased theirs 37 percent to 4.4 million. They may have as many as 25 million in the reserves (of which 5.7 million have had service in the last five years) and 430,000 paramilitary forces. American reserves totaled about 902,200 in 1974.

In *total military expenditures,* the Soviets spent about $143 billion in 1975, and are likely to spend $147 billion in 1976 and $153 billion in 1977 (all in 1974 prices). By comparison, our defense expenditures are $91.2 billion for fiscal year 1976, and $101.1 billion requested for fiscal year 1977. Even if Congress approves this request without a cut, it would mean only a real growth of 2 percent, the first planned real growth since 1968, compared to a real dollar upward trend in Soviet expenditures of about 3 to 5 percent per year. Considering Secretary Rumsfeld's budget projections over the

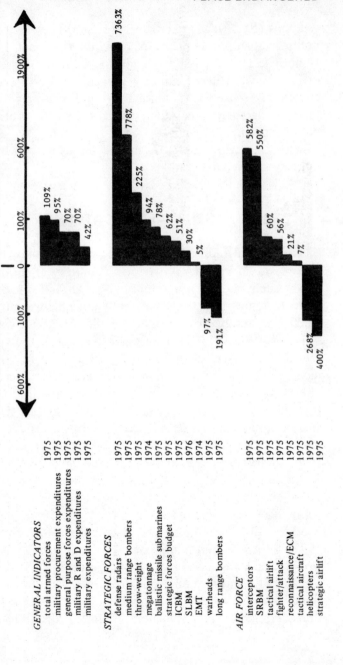

Figure 8.1
U.S.-U.S.S.R. MILITARY BALANCE

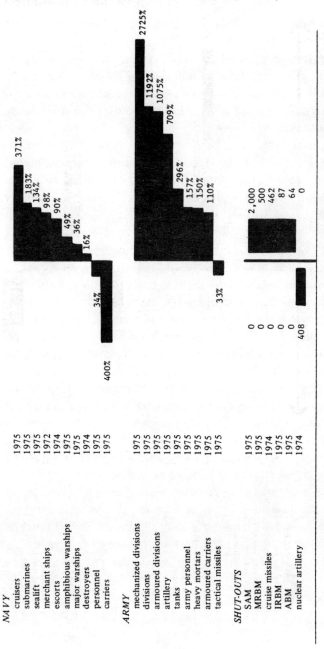

, next five years, we will spend in defense about $200 billion less than the Soviets.

During the years 1968 to 1975, American military expenditures, in constant dollars, fell sharply by 30 percent. The decrease *relative to GNP* was an even more surprising 44 percent; *relative to the federal budget* (outlays), the decrease was 36 percent.

During the same period, *Soviet military expenditures* (in constant dollars) have increased 17 percent. It is estimated that about 15 to 20 percent of the *Soviet GNP* is militarily related, compared to a proposed and decreasing 5.4 percent for America. As former Defense Secretary Schlesinger said, "We have been engaged in the rather peculiar process of reducing our defense budget in real terms while the Soviets have been raising theirs."[4]

But defense totals alone do not tell the whole story. The U.S. defense dollar is swollen by payroll costs. Whereas in 1964, 44 percent of defense expenditures was for payroll, this is projected at 57.3 percent for fiscal year 1977. Between these years, retired military pay has gone from $1.2 to $8.4 billion; active civilian workers from $7.7 to $17 billion; and military pay from $13.5 to $27.4 billion. In stark contrast, Soviet manpower costs are estimated at 15 percent of current military expenditures. They can spend 38 percent more of each dollar on weapons.

Looking at other components of defense, in *military procurement,* the Soviet Union is now outspending us by 95 percent; for *general purpose forces,* they are surpassing us by 70 percent. Considering some details of this disparity, in 1975 the Soviet expenditures exceeded ours by 30 percent for new and more sophisticated aircraft; by 90 percent for procurement of ships and boats; by 100 percent for resources devoted to intercontinental attack; and by 800 percent for territorial defense.

Military research and development is a crucial category; it represents an investment in future qualitative and quantitative changes in the military balance, but here also the Soviets have been outstripping us by about $17 billion to our $10 billion as of 1975 (in FY 1977 dollars). From 1965 to 1975 Soviet R&D (including testing and evaluation) mushroomed about 113 percent while ours dropped 26 percent.

STRATEGIC INDICATORS

The strategic indicators are shown next. These are crucial to the nuclear balance and the Soviet capability to obliterate American forces at one blow. Here, too, the profile of the balance is almost uniformly dismal.

In strategic air *defense radars,* the Soviets have 5,000 to our 67. Given their 850 long- and medium-range bombers which can hit the continental United States, this great disparity is perplexing, unless it is realized that portions of their extensive radar net may be potentially hooked up to·guide their ABMs and thousands of SAMs with ABM potential against our missiles, while we have placed excessive confidence in our ability to absorb a surprise attack and retaliate.

In *medium-range bombers,* they have 500 Tu-16 Badgers and 80 of the new Backfires to our 66 FB-111A, a 778 percent advantage. Their Badgers and Backfires have the capability to fly 4,000 and 6,000 miles, respectively, which means they can drop nuclear bombs on the United States and land in neutral or friendly territory.

In *throw-weight,* The Soviets have approximately 6.5 million pounds to our 2 million pounds, giving them an advantage of 3.25 to 1. This could rise to an overwhelming 6 to 1 if all their older ICBMs are replaced by the new family of ICBMs now being developed. Throw-weight refers to the total weight of a missile's re-entry vehicle containing the warhead, penetration aids, "bus" (if it is a MIRV—multiple independent re-entry vehicle), and so on. Some defense analysts and officials consider throw-weight the most significant indicator of the strategic balance, for it measures not only the size of the warhead that can be delivered but the potential number of MIRV warheads with large yield that can also be carried by one missile. If this is truly a best measure, the Soviets are ahead of us by 225 percent hardly the American superiority that Kissinger alleges.

In *deliverable megatonnage* (explosive power) of nuclear weapons, we are also behind 9,341 megatons to 4,807, or almost 2 to 1. This is partly a result of our disarmament. Our strategic offensive and defensive megatonnage declined 62 percent from 1960 to 1972.

In *ballistic missile submarines* (nuclear and diesel) the Soviets are ahead 73 to 41. They are now shifting their submarine construction to a larger Delta-class submarine which can carry 16 SLBMs, the first of which will be launched this year, and they may be moving to a still larger version which can carry even more missiles. Figure 8.2[5] compares their missile submarines to ours.

In the amount of *expenditures on strategic forces,* which reflects the overall emphasis on the strategic balance, the Soviets were outspending us by at least $12 billion to our 7.4 billion in 1975, or by more than a dangerous 60 percent.[6]

In *ICBMs,* the popular measure of the strategic balance, we are surpassed 1,603 to 1,054, or by 51 percent. Of these, the Soviets have 613 heavy missles to our 54 aged Titans. And this great quantitative ICBM lead is accompanied by sharp qualitative advances. The Soviets are now adding to their missiles at least four completely new types of ICBMs, with improved accuracy and throw-weight. However, we proposed in our 1976-1977 budget to completely close down our

Figure 8.2

OPERATIONAL BALLISTIC MISSILE SUBMARINES

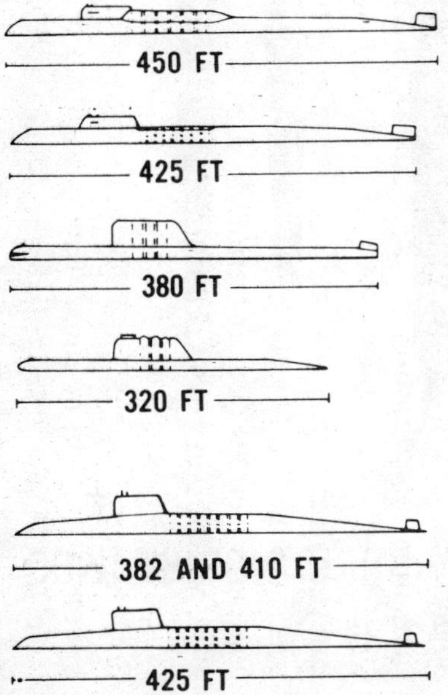

		YEAR OPERATIONAL	PROPULSION		MISSILE
USSR					
D CLASS	450 FT	1973	NUCLEAR	12	SS-N-8
Y CLASS	425 FT	1968	NUCLEAR	16	SS-N-6
H CLASS	380 FT	1960	NUCLEAR	3	SS-N-5
G CLASS	320 FT	1960	DIESEL	3	SS-N-4/5
US					
POLARIS	382 AND 410 FT	1960	NUCLEAR	16	A-3
POSEIDON	425 FT	1971	NUCLEAR	16	C-3

Figure 8.3

COMPARISON OF US AND USSR ICBMs

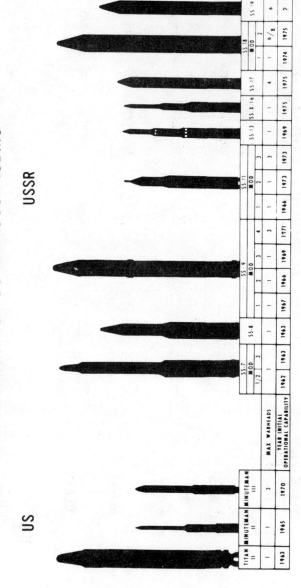

ICBM production lines. Figure 8.3[7] compares Soviet current and new ICBMs to ours. To quote Schlesinger, in 1975 "we are beginning to witness in the Soviet Union the largest initial deployment of improved strategic capabilities in the history of the nuclear competition."[8]

But these new ICBM deployments only represent the surface of Soviet missile research. They have, in addition, about ten newer ICBM systems under development. One year after Schlesinger's comment, Malcolm R. Currie, Director of Defense Research and Engineering, stated before a Senate defense appropriations committee: "We see evidence that the Soviet Union, having gained strategic nuclear parity, is investing increasing resources in efforts to achieve outright superiority, including a search for revolutionary technologies and weapons which could significantly alter the strategic balance."[9] This in the time of détente.

In addition, to their new ICBM systems the Soviets have developed a cold-launch technique for firing ICBMs after they have first been popped out of their silos. This enables rapid reloading of the silos. American ICBMs must be fired in the silo, requiring considerable repair before reloading.

In operational submarine-launched ballistic missiles *(SLBM)*, the Soviets are also now ahead 850 to our 656, and their newest SS-N-8 missiles of which they had 130 in 1975 (and to which they already are developing a successor) outdistance ours by some 2,000 miles. They have a stock of about 1,000 SLBMs.

The Soviets are now testing for their SLBMs an advance over the MIRV, which is a maneuverable warhead (MARV). However, the reliability of our Poseidon SLBM has been seriously compromised through the excessive miniaturization required to carry 10 to 14 MIRV warheads per missile. As of 1973, 58 percent of Poseidon MIRVs had failed their tests. The modification program to overcome this unreliability will

Figure 8.4

COMPARISON OF US AND USSR SLBMs

US   USSR

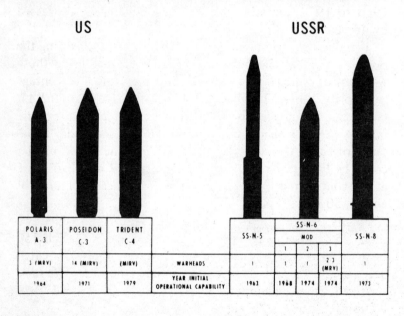

POLARIS A-3	POSEIDON C-3	TRIDENT C-4		SS-N-5	SS-N-6				SS-N-8
					MOD				
					1	2	3		
3 (MRV)	14 (MIRV)	(MIRV)	WARHEADS	1	1	1	2 3 (MRV)		1
1964	1971	1979	YEAR INITIAL OPERATIONAL CAPABILITY	1963	1968	1974	1974		1973

not be completed until 1978. A comparison of U.S. and Soviet SLBMs is shown in Figure 8.4.[10]

In the search for a quantitative indicator of the strategic balance, some defense analysts have proposed equivalent megatonnage *(EMT)* as the best. This measures both the number of strategic nuclear warheads and the yield, taking into account that large warheads waste a certain amount of their explosive power. As of 1974 the Soviets had only a slight edge over us, 4,300 to our 4,100 EMT, a gap which has since widened. But their advantage is of our own doing. From 1960 to 1972, our strategic EMT was unilaterally decreased by 46 percent.

This does not complete the strategic inventory favoring the Soviet Union; at the bottom of Figure 8.1 are listed those weapons of which we have none (and therefore a percentage superiority cannot be given). The Soviets have 12,000 *SAM* (surface-to-air missile) for 9,500 launchers, 462 nuclear *cruise missiles* (SS-N-3 Shaddock), and 64 *ABM* to our none. Thousands of the SAMs are potential ABM, and the cruise missiles could be launched by sub or ship hundreds of miles off shore at the continental United States (the Shaddock has a range of about 450 miles).

Finally, there are two strategic indicators in which we shine. In *long-range bombers* we have 437 B-52s to their 150 Bear (Tu-95) and Bison (Mya-4). However, there is a catch here: their larger number of *medium-range* bombers. We have scrapped every medium-range B-29, B-47, B-36, and B-58 bomber we had.

Then there is the number of strategic *warheads and bombs,* of which we have 8,500. In ICBM/SLBM warheads alone we have 6,794 to their 3,442. This is the favorite measure of the balance used by those who argue that the United States is overwhelmingly ahead of the U.S.S.R., and that therefore we can afford to disarm further. But in the context of the overall military profile as shown in the figure, it is quite clear how misleading is the emphasis on warheads. Moreover, the vast advantage in throw-weight that the Soviets have and their newly capable MIRV missiles (such as the SS-17, SS-19, and the SS-18 Mod 2) promise an end to our warhead superiority.

By the end of 1975, the Soviets had deployed 150 new SS-17, SS-18, and SS-19s. Each SS-19 has about 6 MIRV warheads, and the SS-17 has 4 MIRV warheads apiece. Moreover, they have successfully completed testing at least 7 MIRV warheads for their SS-18. Their annual deployment rate for these new missiles is approaching 200 per year. With their new throw-weight, if the Soviets were to fully deploy these new ICBMs and SLBMs up to the limits permitted by the 1972 SALT I Interim Agreement and MIRV them with yield equivalent to our Minuteman, they could reach a total of 25,000 warheads to our 6,794.

AIR FORCE INDICATORS

The third category of indicators is made up of Air Force nonstrategic weapons.

In *interceptors,* the Soviets outnumber us 2,700 to 396, or a no-contest 582 percent.

What cannot be shown as percentages in the figure are the Soviet's *IRBM* (intermediate-range ballistic missile) and *MRBM* (medium-range ballistic missile) forces, both of which shut us out at 87 and 500 to zero, respectively. The Soviets are now testing a new 2,000-mile IRBM, designated SS-20.

In *SRBM* (short-range ballistic missile) they have 1,170 to our 180.

They also have the better tactical airlift capability with 800 planes (Cub) to our 500, including active and reserve C-130s, and they have 750 reconnaissance and electronic countermeasure aircraft to our 340. We still have the better strategic airlift capability, however, with 300 C-5 and C-141 to their 60. The Soviet airlift of weapons and Cuban troops into Angola in early 1976 showed the surprising capability of two new types of transport, especially the Ilushin-76.

In their favor are *tactical aircraft,* 5,350 to our 5,000 (with an annual production rate now of 930 to our 540); and *fighter/attack aircraft,* 3,590 to our 2,300. And the Soviet Union is constantly improving the quality of her airplanes, and procuring at a 30 percent higher rate than we, while we are relying on older models. At one time in 1974, for example, 35 percent of our tactical planes were not operational due to maintenance problems. Moreover, our air force continues to decline in numbers.

Finally, we greatly exceed the Soviets in *helicopters,* 9,487 (Army and Marines) to their 2,580.

NAVY INDICATORS

Moving now to the fourth category dealing with the Navy, we can note from Figure 8.1 the consistent superiority of the Soviet fleet, supporting the warnings and alarmed cries of our admirals. This is a growing superiority. Moreover, the Soviet fleet comprises a more modern force that is twice as heavily gunned (although the ships are much smaller in size), while our aging ships are overdue for overhaul (a backlog of 71 in 1975, compared to 17 in 1971). The Soviet Union has spent 70 percent more than America in the last ten years on ships and is currently expending 90 percent more. Since 1962 they have built 1,323 ships to our 302. They are now producing 39 surface ships to our 11.

One study by the Naval Ship Engineering Center in Hyattsville, Maryland, points out that the superiority of Soviet warships in firepower over American is bought by sacrificing endurance, electronic sophistication, and crew comforts.

Their ships are built for denying other nations the ability to use the sea. "This design philosophy suggests that these ships are being configured for a pre-emptive first strike in a short, intense conflict."[11]

Turning now to Figure 8.1, with fewer than 500 ships, the *total American Navy* is about what it was in 1939, and *active naval forces* have decreased from about 900 ships in 1968 to 332 in 1975. Total *naval tonnage* has decreased 36 percent from 1964 to 1974, while the Soviets have increased theirs 37 percent. We still have the greater tonnage, however, due mainly to our carriers and the greater range built into our ships.

In *cruisers,* the Soviets have a remarkable 33 to our 7 (active), of which 20 of theirs (to none of ours) are armed with anti-surface-ship cruise missiles.

In *submarines* they far exceed our 115 by 325. They have 253 attack (nuclear and diesel) to our 73, of which 20 have anti-surface-ship cruise missiles. None of ours is so armed. We are constructing new submarines, but so are they at a rate three to four times our number. They now have 11 Delta-class submarines with 4,200-mile SLBMs, and will have 25 by the time our first Trident with a SLBM of comparable range (4,800 miles) is operational. In addition, their current nuclear attack submarines are faster than ours and can launch anti-ship missiles while submerged, a capability we do not have.

In *amphibious warships* they are also ahead 85 to 57.

Even in that area in which a natural American superiority should be expected, *merchant ships,* the Soviets were also far ahead—6,575 to 3,327—in 1972. From 1968 to 1973 our *merchant tonnage* decreased 26 percent, while theirs jumped a sharp 53 percent from 1968 to 1972. In *sealift* capability, they have 2,358 vessels to our 1,009, including merchant marine and 118 Military Sealift Command vessels, the latter down 64 percent since 1965.

In seagoing *escorts* of all types, the Soviets have 110 to our 58.

In the overall category of *major warships,* we again trail 161 to their 219.

And in *destroyers,* they are also ahead 78 to 67 (active). Twenty of theirs are advanced surface-to-surface missile destroyers, of which we have none.

To the American advantage, we have more *naval personnel,* 515,400 to their 386,000, which reflects their smaller ships and our greater logistic and administrative backup.

The only real advantage the American Navy has is its *carriers,* of which we have 13 active, with the retirement of the *Hancock* and *Oriskany* in 1976, to their one Kiev-class carrier plus two helicopter, anti-submarine carrier-cruisers. They have another Kiev-class carrier under construction.

ARMY INDICATORS

Finally, consider the army balance pictured in Figure 8.1. In total number of divisions they have a dominant 168 to our 13 (now being expanded to 16); in *mechanized divisions* they outnumber us 113 to 4; in armored divisions it is 47 to 4. As of 1974, each Soviet mechanized division had 255 medium and 19 light tanks to our 216 and 54 (in Europe; 27 elsewhere), respectively; their armored division had 60 medium guns to our 54, and more heavies as of 1973. Their mechanized division also had more heavy guns as of 1973, and in 1974 they had 72 guns to our 54. In sum, there is not that much weapons difference between the divisional establishments to account for the huge disparity in numbers.

It is not surprising, therefore, that they should have 40,000 *tanks* to our 10,100—an impressive and alarming disparity. Moreover, of their number, 2,500 are heavy tanks, of which we have none, and they have 34,500 medium tanks to our 8,500. Their tanks are generally qualitatively better than our most widely used 1960 models. Half of our first-line tanks may not be operational. Currently, the Soviets are producing 3,000 tanks annually to our 540.

In conventional *artillery,* the Soviets have 17,000 pieces to our 2,100, and theirs has the longer range. Moreover, they are producing 1,200 to our 170 a year. In anti-tank missiles, they have 6,000 to our 2,400.

In *heavy mortars,* they also outgun us 7,500 to 3,000, and in *armored carriers* they have 40,000 to our 19,000.

Overall, in *army personnel,* they have 2.5 million to our 986,100 (including Marines).

Finally, the American Army is sadly underequipped. It has only 51 percent of the equipment needed to modernize and sustain its combat forces. For example, the Army has 78 percent of the helicopters and 51 percent of the troop carriers required to equip 16 active and 8 reserve divisions.

The public tends to view such a disparity in Army weapons and personnel as insignificant, since America's undeniable industrial capability can come to the rescue and mass produce the weapons needed if war breaks out. However, with today's weapons, the time for mobilization may not be available. According to Lieutenant General Orwin C. Talbott, "If we lose the first battle there probably will not be enough military power left for a second battle because of the high rate of attrition in modern war."[12]

Returning to the comparisons in Figure 8.1, we are ahead in two areas. We have 20,000 to their 15,000 *tactical missiles,* and 408 self-propelled nuclear *artillery pieces* to their zero (our only shut-out). This is due to our attempt to overcome the conventional military superiority of the Warsaw Pact countries against NATO by tactical nuclear weapons.

Thus we have the current military balance. Clearly, considering the whole military profile, we are sadly eclipsed. The

United States is ahead on only 8 out of 48 indicators, and as Figure 8.1 shows, we generally lead by narrow margins whereas the Soviets lead by wide margins.

But those comparisons are quantitative and they are matching indicators and systems on a one-to-one basis, whereas Soviet and American missions and roles are not the same and the geographic and political factors affecting military capabilities differ markedly. A recent Library of Congress study assessed such asymmetries and concluded that our only military superiority which is "an assured asset" is in amphibious landing forces and carriers. However, the Soviet Union has an "important" superiority in heavy and total ICBMs, army personnel, divisions, main battle tanks, armored carriers, tube artillery, SSM cruisers, SSM destroyers, attack submarines, and fighter/attack (excluding carrier-based) aircraft.[13]

In addition, the study appraised U.S. ends and means, comparing available military capability to American foreign policy goals. Serious shortcomings were shown, which are as follows:[14]

Strategic nuclear problems

    postlaunch survivability of ICBMs
    postlaunch survivability of bombers
    defense of U.S. population and production base

NATO-related problems

    active army small compared with global commitments
    key assets extremely concentrated
    absence of ABM defense in Europe
    cracks in NATO alliance
    readiness/responsiveness of U.S. reserve components

Naval combat problems

    protect U.S. shipping/reinforce NATO

    navy small compared with global commitments
    surface combatants exposed to short-range missiles
    ASW unable to cope with large-scale submarine threat
    amphibious lift insufficient for landing forces

Strategic mobility problems

    airlift insufficient to move ready reserves rapidly
    sealift depends on foreign-flag carriers

In sum, while certain American quantitative inferiorities need not cause concern since they are related to U.S.-Soviet asymmetries, there are several inferiorities which reflect crucial inadequacies in our defenses, both on a one-to-one comparison of those weapons which make a difference strategically or conventionally, such as ICBMs and SSM cruisers, and in terms of American goals.

Those comparisons notwithstanding, however, many feel that we are so technically superior that these inferiorities can be easily rectified if we so desire. However, consider both Soviet technological growth and their latest weapons initiatives.

What is not shown on the Figure 8.1 are the advances the Soviet Union is making in building the technological base underlying her phenomenal military growth. According to Director Currie of Defense Research and Engineering in his February, 1976, statement before Congress, the Soviet Union has gained parity with the United States in high-yield nuclear weapons (and has made several unique developments), while taking the lead in high-pressure physics, welding, titanium fabrication, high-frequency radio wave propagation, magneto-hydrodynamic power generation, anti-ship missiles, chemical warfare, and artillery technology. The comparison is uncertain for high-energy lasers, and mixed for aerodynamics. The United States still retains the lead in integrated-circuit fabrication, computers, high-bypass-ratio turbofans, air-to-air missiles, numerically controlled machine tools, avionics, composite materials, inertial instrumentation, precision-guided weapons, and satellite-borne sensor technology.

Moreover, what is also not shown in the chart are the new qualitative initiatives that the Soviets are taking in strategic and conventional forces, which reflect their accelerating technological capability and military investments. The most important of these are as follows:

—four new ICBM systems many times the throw-weight of our Minuteman and three of which have a MIRV capability;

—a new ICBM cold-launch technique, enabling the Soviets to put much larger missiles in their silos and rapidly reload them after firing;

—construction and modification of hardened silos;

—construction of large numbers of hardened command and control centers;

—development of two land-mobile ICBM systems (one is the SS-X-16);

—new, more effective guidance systems with onboard computers, including a stellar-guidance systems for their new SS-N-8 SLBM with a pace of improvement in missile accuracy much greater than thought possible;

—a new SLBM (SS-N-8) of 4,200-nautical-mile range, which is the equivalent of our new Trident missile scheduled to come into service in mid-1979;

—improvement of and the testing of MIRVs for the SS-N-6 SLBM deployed on Yankee-class submarines;

—testing of a maneuverable SLBM warhead;

—two new types of Delta-class submarines, including a lengthened super Delta capable of carrying 16 missiles;

—new variable-geometry wing bomber, the Backfire, which is a versatile multipurpose aircraft capable of nuclear strike, conventional, attack, anti-ship, reconnaissance, and electronic warfare missions;

—research and development of two new ABM systems;

—two new classes of satellites for ocean surveillance and perhaps targeting information, as well as a space program enabling them to launch more than eight times the American military space-craft in 1975;

—new all-weather interceptors, such as the Foxbat (MIG-25) with new air-to-air missiles, and the Flagon E (SU-15);

—research and development of new over-the-horizon radar;

—production and deployment of the M-1970 medium tank;

—new fighting vehicle (BMD), which is air-droppable, amphibious, and equivalent to a light tank;

—new self-propelled artillery (122mm/152mm);

—new tactical SAMs (SA-8);

—new Hind A helicopter, which carries 57mm rocket pods or anti-tank missiles, or 8 to 16 troops;

—new Kiev-class carrier of 900 feet and 35,000 tons when fully equipped;

—new Kuril-class V/STOL carrier;

—new Kara-class cruiser, which is heavily armed with impressive arrays of anti-ship and anti-air missiles, plus anti-submarine sensors and weapons;

—new Krivak-class destroyers, also similarly armed;

—new Amga-class missile support ship;

—new Ropucha-class LST:

—new SU-19 (Fencer A) fighter bomber, designed to specifically engage ground troops;

—new MIG-23 (Flogger) fighter, with interceptor, interdiction, and close air support ability;

—new SU-17 (Fitter C) fighter bomber, which is ideally suited to ground attack;

—new V/STOL fighter.

President Ford and Secretary Kissinger have assured the public that détente has not weakened us, that we maintain the edge over the Soviet Union. The evidence does not support them.

Détente has not meant simply a restraint of American military power consistent with mutual U.S.-Soviet arms control, nor American superiority. It has not even meant parity. *It has meant dangerous inferiority.*

Détente has been an unrelieved slide into a second place where Soviet weapons outnumber ours by two, three, four, and even five or more to one. This bleak picture is hardly relieved by reference to our superiority in warheads, long-range bombers, carriers, or nuclear artillery, for these do not make up for our inferior defense and strategic expenditures, research and development, medium bombers, throw-weight, subs, ICBMs, fighter/attack aircraft, warships divisions, tanks, and artillery. In total military effort and overall establishment we are far behind, and the gap is increasing rapidly. And our ability to accomplish our own foreign policy goals, even as now limited, is in serious doubt.

This deterioration has had little publicity. Yet it so imperils freedom that we must scrutinize the nature and change in this military gap; the trends must be sharply defined. Again the computer can help us.

First, we should ask a question which will give more meaning to this computer analysis. Why have we been disarming while the Soviets surge ahead? This is the concern of the next chapter.

NOTES

1. SAC Air Force Base, Grand Forks, North Dakota, July 25, 1974.

2. June 3, 1974.

3. The scale is in logarithms of the percentage, in order to accommodate the very large percentages and still discriminate the differences among the percentages less than a hundred.

4. James R. Schlesinger, *Annual Defense Department Report FY 1976 and FY 197T,* February 5, 1975, p. I-10.

5. From the Statement of General George S. Brown, Chairman of the Joint Chiefs of Staff, on the "United States Military Posture for FY 1976" before the Committee on Defense of the Senate Committee on Appropriations (n.d.).

6. The Soviet figure is an underestimate, perhaps by as much as 50 percent. However, I could find no updated data consistent with recent re-estimates of Soviet military expenditures.

7. Ibid.

8. Schlesinger, op. cit., p. I-5.

9. *Baltimore Sun,* February 4, 1976, p. 2.

10. Brown, op. cit.

11. *The New York Times,* August 11, 1975.

12. *The New York Times,* July 9, 1975, p. 2.

13. John M. Collins and John Steven Chwat, *The United States/ Soviet Military Balance: A Frame of Reference for Congress* (The Library of Congress, January 21, 1976).

14. Ibid., p. 27, Figure 10.

The Détente MADmen

9

Fifteen years more of a deterioration of our position in the world such as we have experienced since World War II would find us reduced to a Fortress America in a world in which we had become largely irrelevant.

—Henry Kissinger, *The Necessity for Choice,* 1960

Détente II has led to an **American inferiority in arms, an** unprecedented unilateral disarming process at a time when Soviet leaders have not slackened their animosity toward our fundamental values. While we reduce our weapons they maneuver and prepare for the final defeat of the West, now no less than during the Cold War. Why, then, have we been disarming?

Numerous reasons can be given. Vietnam has soured many Americans on globalism and "policing the world," encouraging isolationism and a sharp reduction in arms. A new generation of leaders, unaware of the crises and fears of the late 1940s and 1950s, suspicious of Cold War rhetoric, are now less concerned about communism than about domestic and environmental problems. A large bureaucracy involved in the welfare and service activities—and their constituencies—that now dominate the government are increasingly able to defeat the Pentagon in toe-to-toe budget battles. Anti-militarism grew into a liberal-welfare ideology during the Vietnam War and now overwhelms pro-defense voices. These and other reasons can be given.

But the policy and implementation of détente (I and II) bear the major responsibility for our inferiority. The impact of détente on our military power has been along four dimensions. *The first is the euphoria that détente and its good words have aroused.* Détente has eliminated the Cold War, sharply reduced tensions, and insured peace, or so many believe. The Soviets are no longer enemies—they are our "competitors."

With this muting of the Cold War on our side has come a depreciation of the ideological struggle. Communism is no longer the inhumane, barbaric creed enslaving the peoples of China, Russia, the Ukraine, Rumania, Hungary, Latvia, Estonia, and so on. Rather our "systems" are simply different and our policies are based on "divergent national interests." In the eyes of détente, the United States and the Soviet Union are symmetrical, two nations with dissimilar interests and beliefs which must learn to get along and cooperate for their own good and that of the world.

Under the influence of détente, America has lost its sense of danger. It is no longer sure of who the enemy is—whether communism, poverty, or capitalism. It is unfashionable to be anti-communist, to worry about defense, or to fault communists in movies or on television.

Lulled by détente into a false sense of security and national interest, Congress, which is after all still responsive to the grass roots, each year decreases the defense budget in real terms. Why should money that is badly needed for domestic programs go to military hardware when we now have harmonious relations with our competitors? Of course we must be on guard, but we have enough defense for that—after all, "we have enough bombs to destroy all mankind."

Even when a congressional committee bestirs itself to warn of the astounding Soviet strategic drive, it is ignored by the media. For example, the Joint Committee on Atomic Energy (among whose members are Senators Symington, Montoya, and Tunney and Representatives McCormack and Moss, none of whom is notably pro-defense) stated in a unanimous report that the U.S.S.R. is overtaking the United States in the quality of its nuclear weapons, is ahead in all other areas of nuclear weapons, and is conducting "a massive research-and-development effort" regarding new nuclear weapons. Moreover, it pointed out that *the Soviet Union is developing a first-strike capability that could destroy most American retaliatory forces, and the threat to use her invulnerable reserve forces against American cities would deter a suicidal American retaliation.* Additional details were also given on ten arms programs the Soviets were pursuing aggressively (all of which were described in Chapter 8). This crucial report was ignored by the press until Edward O'Brien, chief of the *St. Louis Globe-Democrat* Washington bureau, heard about it and reported its findings. He was the first newsman to sign a receipt log for a copy of the report from committee staffers; two members of the Soviet embassy had signed before him.[1]

Détente had to be sold to the American people, and to do this a halo of glowing words was created. Now the halo has become reality. The Cold War rages, but only the Soviets are fighting it. Their victory may come by default.

The second dimension of détente's impact on American power has been the one-sided arms-control agreements entered into with the Soviet Union, especially the SALT I and Vladivostok accords. Although hailed by the managers of Détente II as a major breakthrough in limiting strategic armaments, the consequence has been to restrict American strategic development and deployment while the Soviets have continued their rapid buildup with hardly a pause.[2]

These agreements were made with a view toward their effect on détente; they were good-faith tickets indicating a Soviet faith in détente. There was thus less concern with the impact of these agreements on the military balance and an ominous lack of concern for making them watertight.[3] As Dr. James E. Dornan, Jr., Chairman of the Department of Politics at Catholic University, put it:

> The history of the SALT negotiations and accords [has] shown Kissinger to be less than satisfactory as the steward of American strategic interests. In order to regain ·American military security, President Ford and future administrations and the Congress must seek to overcome the clear nuclear superiority which SALT I has bestowed on the Soviets.[4]

No matter if the Soviets have been helped by these agreements and at most follow their letter while violating their spirit. Americans typically take to heart the spirit of such accords. We can hardly invest in strategic arms or increase our inventory or prepare new weapons for a possible Soviet breakthrough when, after all, we have signed a treaty to control them. Thus, to the fine halo of détente is added the admirable spirit of SALT. Only an old Cold Warrior can push arms under these circumstances. Few have sought this stigma.

The third and fourth dimensions along which détente has plunged us into military inferiority involve the acceptance of

*the mutual assured destruction (MAD) doctrine and the
uncritical belief in an action-reaction arms race.*

Armaments are not just produced and deployed in response to fears, insecurities, and foreign threats. Policy
choices are many and conflicting; a political process of deci-
sionmaking with many bureaucratic twists and turns must
work itself out. There are alternative costs of separate armament programs; there are diverse armament systems to develop—not all of which can be supported even by the most
defense-oriented. There are domestic pressures against the
defense dollar, associated with anti-militaristic attitudes or
competing interest groups. The choices that are made, therefore, must have some guiding spirit, some orientation which
helps decide on what to research, what to build, and what to
deploy where. This is obvious.

Less appreciated is the need, too, for some orientation for
interpreting the military choices of the Soviets. A framework
is required within which to decide what to do about our
military power and how to perceive Soviet power, and this
has been provided by the doctrine of mutual assured destruction and the action-reaction theory.

Since World War II, American strategic doctrines have
undergone several alterations in response to the Soviet threat,
our growing nuclear stockpile and that of the Soviets, and the
influence of one school of civil-defense analysts after
another.

Immediately following World War II we demobilized and
returned to a doctrine of war mobilization—a belief that
America was still distant enough from potential enemies and
so economically powerful that we could keep a minimum
military establishment. There would be time and space to
mobilize in case of war or extreme danger.

The Iranian crisis of 1946, the Czechoslovakian communist
coup, the Berlin Blockade, the fall of China in 1948, and the
successful Soviet atomic bomb test in 1949 forced a reassess-

ment of our strategic doctrine. Any new doctrine would gain sustenance and direction, however, from major changes in American foreign policy.

In June, 1947, George Kennan (then head of the Department of State's Policy Planning Staff) published his famous article in *Foreign Affairs* defining the policy of containment, which became our bedrock foreign policy until Nixon's "Structure of Peace" in 1969—the beginning of détente. Containment was implemented through the formation of NATO in 1949 and the numerous multilateral and bilateral defense alliances erected around the Soviet Union.

Moreover, in 1947 the Truman Doctrine—by which we agreed to help any free nation struggling against foreign aggression or subversion—gave American support to collective security. This doctrine underlay American involvement in Korea in 1950, the stationing of troops with NATO in Europe in 1951, the Lebanon landing of 1958, the Bay of Pigs fiasco of 1961, the Dominican Republic intervention of 1965, and, of course, Vietnam. The Truman Doctrine rode out the first two years of the Nixon Administration, but was finally replaced by the Nixon Doctrine. We will now help only those freedom fighters who help themselves.

Containment was transformed into détente; the Truman Doctrine was transformed into the Nixon Doctrine. These basic foreign policies and doctrines provide the background against which various strategic doctrines developed. In reaction to the loss of China and the Soviet atomic bomb, in 1950 the National Security Council issued its famous document, NSC 68, which constituted a total reassessment of American military policy and advocated an immediate military mobilization in the hope of avoiding war and inducing a change in the Soviet system. Future war was to be deterred by rearmament. This doctrine could not be put into operation, however, until the outbreak of the Korean War. Then for three years we engaged in a crash military buildup, almost quadrupling our defense budget, from $13 billion to $50.4 billion, for the fiscal years ending in 1950 and 1953 respectively.

However, NSC 68 was based on the belief that we were in a crisis situation that demanded action and that expenditures on arms could be reduced after the crisis passed. President Eisenhower was elected to office in 1952, by which time it was becoming clear that we were involved in a protracted struggle with communism and that we had to prepare our defenses for a long haul. Yet competing domestic demands were emerging and it appeared that a crisis mobilization defense program could not be long sustained. This, in addition to the death of Stalin in 1953 and an apparent thaw in Soviet foreign policy, led to the "New Look" of the Eisenhower Administration—an attempt to balance domestic demands with an assumed constant communist threat.

The New Look embodied a strategic doctrine that placed primary emphasis on our nuclear weapons, which became known as the doctrine of "massive retaliation" after a 1954 speech in which Secretary of State Dulles declared that we might respond massively to communist aggression. In addition to this highly publicized aspect, the New Look also made provisions for a lower military budget, the assembling of a U.S. mobile strategic reserve, the development of an effective continental defense system, and the preparation of a mobilization base for general war.

By 1955, the Soviets appeared to counterbalance American superiority with long-range bombers (the "bomber gap" period) and an accumulation of thermonuclear weapons. Thus the "balance of terror" emerged. It was perceived that neither side could attack the other without receiving a devastating blow in return. Moreover, strategic forces no longer seemed capable of deterring limited war and there was an increasing consideration of the need for a limited-war capability. The military budget, however, was kept fairly level.

With the Soviet Sputnik and first ICBM in 1957, a possible missile gap favoring the Soviets became a hot political issue (the "missile gap" period), but there was no change in strategic doctrine until Kennedy was elected in 1960. After a year of consideration, Kennedy began to implement a new tactical policy called "flexible response" and a strategic "second-strike counterforce" doctrine. Flexible response consisted of reducing the reliance on nuclear weapons and building up our conventional-force capability to meet many different kinds of aggression at different levels. It was considered the sophisticated analyst's alternative to massive retaliation. Second-strike Counterforce, first enunciated by Defense Secretary McNamara in the early 1960s, was a strategy of developing our capacity to absorb a surprise Soviet blow at our nuclear weapons and still be able to retaliate against Soviet military forces and targets. This doctrine required superior military forces and contributed a strategic initiative to our military buildup already underway as a result of a perceived missile gap in the late 1950s.

By 1965, however, McNamara had rethought the problem of deterring nuclear war. He proposed a new doctrine called "assured destruction capability," by which our nuclear offensive weapons (ICBMs, SLBMs, and SAC bombers) would be able to ride out a surprise attack *(first strike)* and retaliate sufficiently on the Soviet Union to destroy it as a viable society. By then deterrence was seen as depending on the ability to survive a first strike and utterly devastate the other's cities and industrial capacity. When both sides have this capability it is called "mutual assured destruction," or MAD for short.

According to McNamara, our strategic forces would need no capability other than that contributed to MAD. The only justification for strategic expenditures, then, would be their contribution to limiting damage to the United States, or to

our ability to retaliate (the application of McNamara's noto-
rious "cost effectiveness" criteria). Another assumption that
was very much a part of this doctrine was that MAD created
a stable strategic balance which minimized the risk of nuclear
war and that Soviet leaders would follow this doctrine as
their strategic analysis matured.

Under the banner of assured destruction, the Johnson
Administration began to reduce American strategic forces.
Hundreds of strategic bombers and missiles were scrapped,
the sizes of our warheads were decreased, the strategic budget
was cut, and a decision was made to level off the number of
Minuteman missiles at 1,000 and SLBMs at 656. (Did you
ever wonder why the number of American ICBMs and SLBMs
has remained the same from 1967 to today?) The reason was
that "excessive" strategic power was unnecessary because the
United States had forsworn a first strike against the U.S.S.R.
All we needed, therefore, was a retaliatory capability.

MAD is still the doctrine of Détente II. We still keep our
strategic forces reduced to a level we believe sufficient
(Nixon's "sufficiency") to retaliate if we are attacked. The
Soviets have overtaken us partly for this reason.

Recall that in McNamara's day the Soviet strategists were
simply "naïve" about nuclear weapons and deterrence. In
time they would believe in MAD. Under Détente II, however,
MAD has taken on new meaning: a belief in a truly mutual
assured destruction has been transformed into a *faith* in the
other side following the same rules.

Have the Soviets accepted MAD? There "is no Soviet
equivalent of 'assured destruction,' much less any acceptance
of mutuality in enjoying such a principle."[5] They have
always felt that nuclear weapons were to be used in war and
that one should be prepared to use them to the fullest. Their
strategic doctrine has emphasized one superordinate point:
be superior to your enemy. Thus, strategically the Soviets

were behind until about 1968, then there was a short-lived parity, and now they have forged ahead. *While we emphasize war-avoidance, they configure their forces for waging war.*

Perhaps the number of weapons scrapped best exemplifies the two doctrines. From 1946 to 1974 we have built and *scrapped* 1,210 ICBMs, 544 SLBMs, and around 1,400 bombers; at the same time the Soviets have scrapped 11 ICBMs, 15 bombers, and no SLBMs.

The uncritical acceptance of MAD by the Nixon and Ford administrations and the projection onto our worst enemy of our own judgments have led in part to our current critical state.

In addition to MAD there is one other reason for our disarmament, which is a long-standing theory in international relations. It is simply this: Arms races involve an upward-spiraling action-reaction sequence. One side builds a battleship, which the other sees as a threat; it also builds a battleship for its security, but just to be on the safe side, it builds a second one as well. The first side, now feeling threatened itself, builds a second ship, and also a third. Now the other side is again threatened and ... Whether ships, bombers, missiles, submarines, or defense expenditures, the logic is the same. Action and reaction.

The belief is that nations actually become trapped in such a process, which grips them in a race that can only lead to increased tensions, hostility, and war. To reduce tension and the risk of war, therefore, we must break this self-reinforcing vicious cycle.

Kissinger firmly believes in this theory of arms races. We need simply to allow the Soviets to attain parity so that we no longer "threaten them," and then "break the momentum of ever increasing levels of armaments"[6] through arms-control agreements and unilateral restraint. This will control the arms race and still provide MAD stability, thus minimizing the risk of nuclear war—the ultimate détente goal.

Therefore the MAD doctrine in conjunction with this action-reaction theory of arms races largely explains our strategic weapons choices, investments, and disarmament.

Today the Soviets are superior. They now appear to be moving close to a first-strike capability, or at least there is evidence of this (which I will consider in Chapter 11). The data in the preceding chapter also revealed, at least as far as percentages were concerned, that the Soviets seemed to be increasing their armaments in response to our decreases. Is this not sufficient to junk MAD and the action-reaction theory? "Until the adherents of unilateral disarmament can persuade the Soviets that they should reduce their massive armaments to the level of necessity, the NATO nations must abide by the lesson of history—unnecessarily large forces are intended for aggressive action."[7]

Yet the two trends continue—the United States decreases, the Soviet Union increases. We will look at these two trends in detail in the next chapter.

NOTES

1. *St. Louis Globe-Democrat,* August 6, 1975, p. 10A.
2. Donald G. Brennan, "When SALT Hit the Fan," *National Review,* June 23, 1972; and Phyllis Schlafly and Chester Ward, *Kissinger on the Couch* (New Rochelle: Arlington House, 1975).
3. John Newhouse, *Cold Dawn: The Story of SALT* (New York: Holt, Rinehart, & Winston, 1973).
4. "Détente and the Pending Strategic Crisis," American Conservative Union Education and Research Institute, Washington, D.C.
5. John Erickson, "Soviet Military Power," *Strategic Review* (Special Supplement), Vol. 1 (Spring 1973), pp. iii-127.
6. Secretary Kissinger's statement before the Senate Committee on Foreign Relations on September 19, *The Department of State Bulletin,* Vol. LXXI (October 14, 1974), p. 513.
7. *Jane's Fighting Ships 1975-76.*

Power in Retreat

10

> *The USSR ... has embarked upon a massive program of major strategic force improvements and deployments which, if not constrained by the negotiating process or balanced by major US arms initiatives, will result in serious superiority over the United States in the years ahead.*
>
> —General George S. Brown,
> Chairman, Joint Chiefs of Staff,
> *United States Military Posture for FY 1976*

My static comparison of the military balance in Chapter 8 does not show the essential trends and increasing gaps. We must look at the changing balance through the years to discern the trends that point to a Soviet superiority.

As a help in viewing the dynamics of the military balance, Chart 10.1 provides a historical overview of the time frame to be covered. By comparing changing trends with this chart,

Chart 10.1

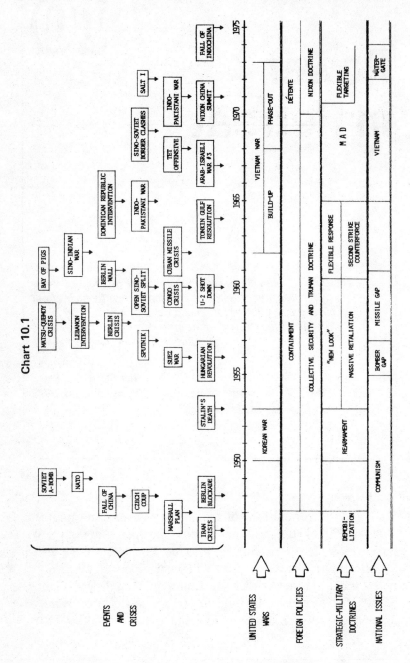

one can detect some of the underlying events, issues, and policy shifts responsible for the change in direction of the balance. For example, the Korean and Vietnam wars have had a definite impact on U.S. military trends. Moreover, 1968, the year of the Vietcong Tet offensive, was the high point for many trends, after which a steep decline clearly accelerated by détente set in. Many of the policies and doctrines shown in the chart were described in the preceding chapter.

GENERAL INDICATORS

We turn now to the military trends shown in Figures 10.1-5. Those portions of the figures measuring Soviet superiority are shown in black.

Figures 10.1A-D plot the trends in the general indicators of the balance, measuring the changes in the overall force levels and military expenditures. Figure 10.1A shows the total armed forces for the United States and the Soviet Union. The effect of the Korean and Vietnam wars on American force levels are evident in the plot. Current force levels are the lowest since the Korean War, while the Soviets are increasing after a period of decline (1955-1965). The sharpest increase for the Soviets over the whole period was in the last year, during détente.[1]

Figure 10.1B presents the change in relative military expenditures. The Soviets surpassed us in 1972, and have been increasing the gap since.[2] Again we can see the influence of both the Korean and Vietnam wars, and the precipitous decline since the 1968 Tet offensive. It should be noted that this is the trend in real expenditures, with the inflation effect removed. The American trend is tilted upward from 1955 to 1975 only because military retirement pay is

(text continued on page 100)

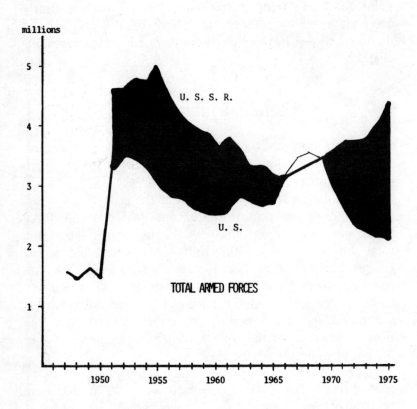

Figure 10.1A

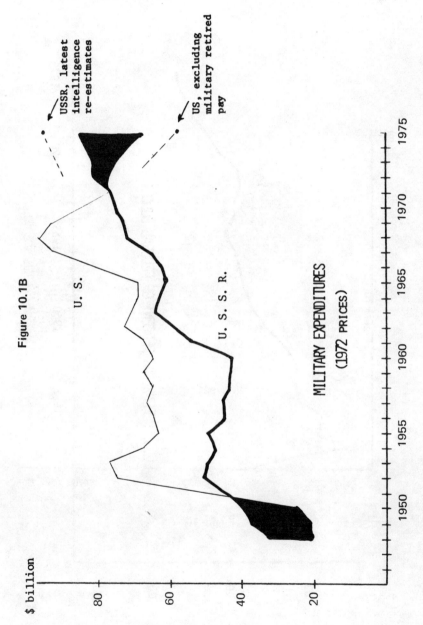

Figure 10.1B

MILITARY EXPENDITURES
(1972 PRICES)

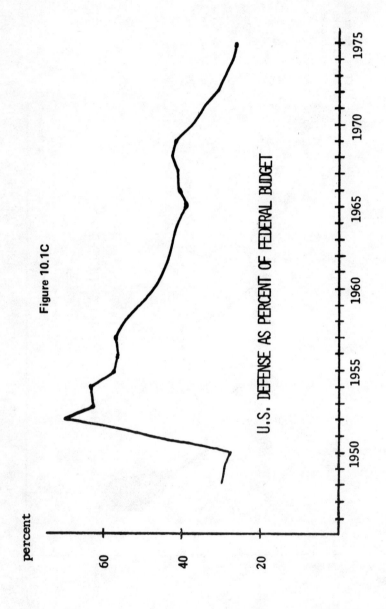

Figure 10.1C

U.S. DEFENSE AS PERCENT OF FEDERAL BUDGET

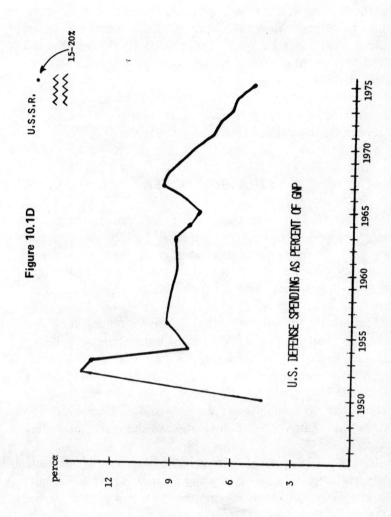

Figure 10.1D

included. If these pensions were excluded, the 1975 expenditure figure would be lower than that for 1955.

Figures 10.1C and D reveal the defense budget in relation to the federal budget and to GNP. Regarding the federal budget, defense now takes the smallest percentage since before World War II. And relative to GNP, defense has the smallest percentage since the demobilization period before the Korean War.

Note that 1969 is the first of the Nixon years and détente ("Structure of Peace"). In each chart a steep slide, if not the steepest, begins in 1968 or 1969.

STRATEGIC POWER

Figures 10.2A-G plot the trends in strategic power. Figure 10.2A displays the relative strategic budgets in constant dollars. This figure alone exposes the emphasis on strategic systems. It also explains why the Soviets are moving into strategic dominance with new and advanced strategic weapons and technologies.

Figure 10.2B displays the relative trends in ICBM launchers, and Figure 10.2C the SLBMs. Relative ballistic-missile submarines are shown in Figure 10.2D. In these three figures the numbers remain constant for the United States from 1967 to the present, a policy decision made in the belief that these limits would suffice for deterrence (the policy of assured destruction discussed in the preceding chapter).

Figure 10.2E presents the relative numbers of medium- and long-range bombers excluding 80 new Soviet 6,000-mile Backfires). Soviet medium-range bombers can hit the United States and then land in neutral or friendly territory such as Cuba. Moreover, U.S. medium-range B-36, B-47, and B-58

(text continued on page 108)

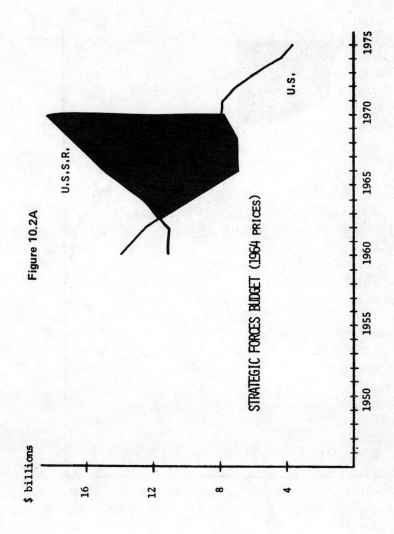

Figure 10.2A

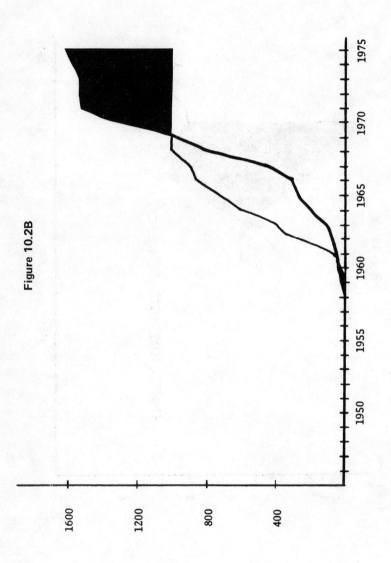

Figure 10.2B

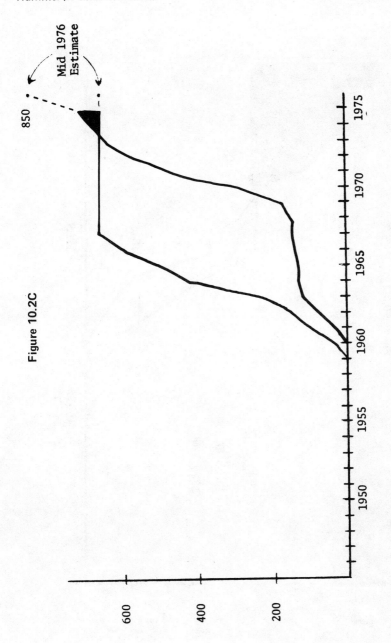

Figure 10.2C

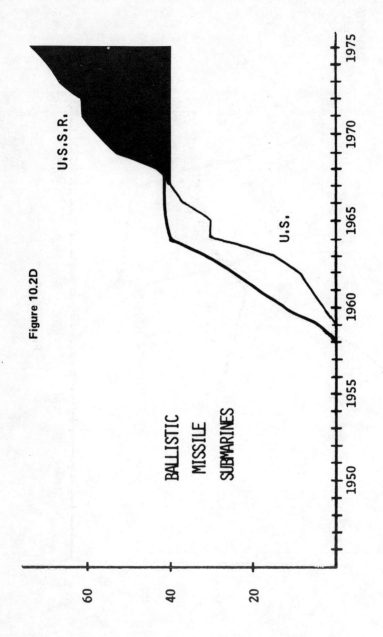

Figure 10.2D

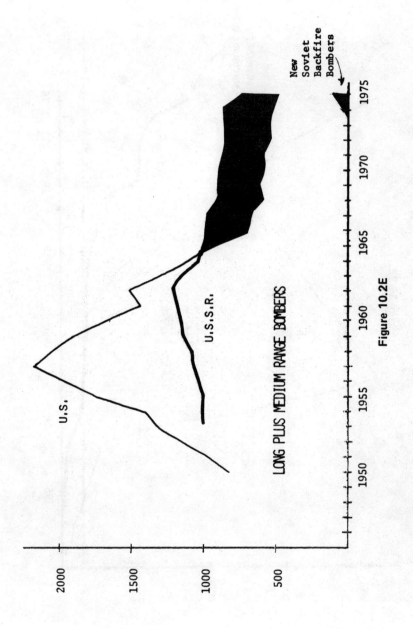

Figure 10.2E

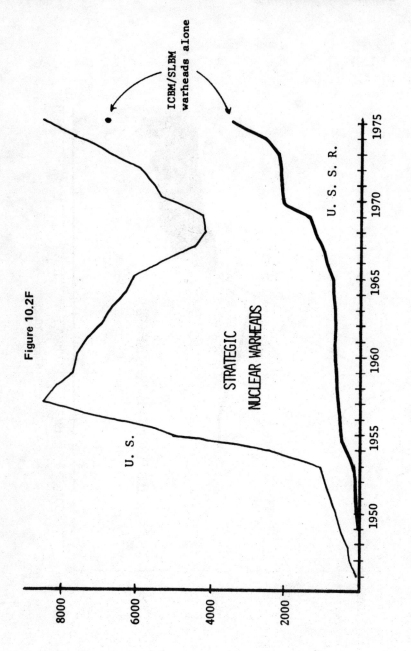

Figure 10.2F

ICBM/SLBM warheads alone

STRATEGIC
NUCLEAR WARHEADS

U. S.

U. S. S. R.

8000

6000

4000

2000

1950   1955   1960   1965   1970   1975

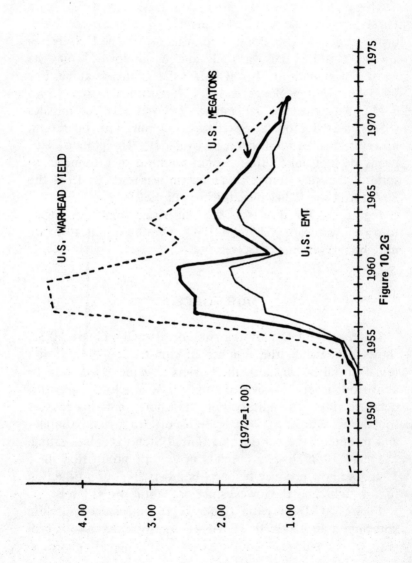

Figure 10.2G

bombers were considered strategic until phased out with the growth in our long-range B-52 force.

The plot of warheads (force loadings) shown in Figure 10.2F has been the prime example of "great American superiority" and the "U.S.-dominated arms race." The U.S. figures are for ICBM/SLBM warheads and bomb loads, while the latest Soviet data are for ICBM/SLBM warheads alone. For 1975 the United States had 6,794 warheads to the Soviet 3,442. With the new generation of Soviet MIRVed missiles (SS-17, SS-18 Mod. 2, SS-19) now coming into operation, however, this gap will soon be overcome. The plots of warheads do not take into account warhead megatonnage. In spite of the quantitative advantage in warheads, in 1974 the Soviet lead was 9,341 megatons to our 4,807.

Figure 10.2G discloses the American trends in megatonnage, warhead yield and EMT. On these indicators we have been disarming ourselves.

AIR FORCE

Figures 10.3A-D plot the Air Force trends. Figure 10.3A shows that while the number of our tactical aircraft has remained fairly constant, the Soviets have increased theirs to above our level. However, Figure 10.3B discloses the sharp decrease in our military air transport and interceptor squadrons. Our capability to transport troops and supplies and to defend the continental United States is deteriorating.

Figure 10.3C displays trends in aircraft production since 1946. We now produce few new bombers and our production of new fighters is the lowest since pre-World War II levels.

Figure 10.3D presents trends in reconnaissance satellite launchings. In 1962, the Soviets undertook a vigorous program of launchings which they have maintained after surpass-

(text continued on page 113)

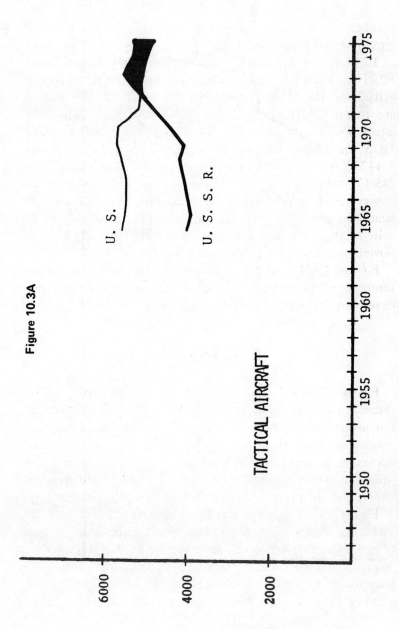

Figure 10.3A

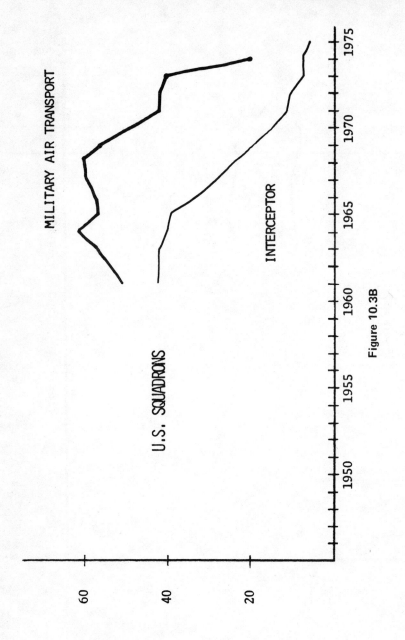

Figure 10.3B

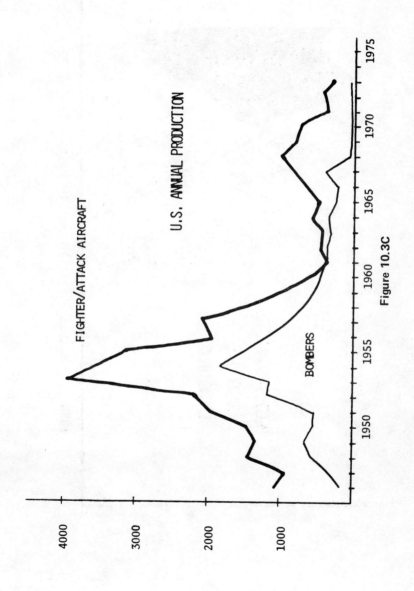

Figure 10.3C

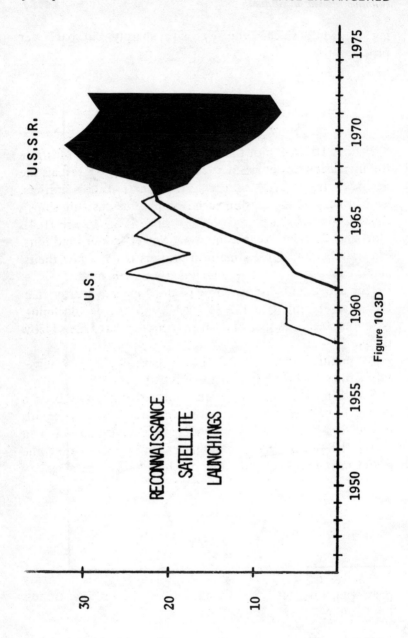

Figure 10.3D

ing us, while since 1966 we have sharply cut back our program.

NAVY

Figures 10.4A-E plot the relative naval trends and illustrate the increasing Soviet naval strength. Figure 10.4A reveals the declining trend in American active naval forces (carriers, submarines, other warships, and amphibious assault ships); this decline has sharply accelerated since 1968. Figure 10.4B plots the changing balance between Soviet cruisers and ours. The number of active American cruisers is far below theirs, and even when the reserve is included we are behind.

Our active and reserve force of destroyers is greater than theirs, as presented in Figure 10.4C, but sharply declining. Now our total number of active destroyers has fallen below theirs.

As pictured in Figure 10.4D, we have always had fewer submarines, and the gap remains about the same.

Surprisingly to me, since the United States has been a dominant naval and commercial power, are the relative trends in the Soviet and American merchant marine uncovered in Figure 10.4E. If these trends have continued, by now the Soviet merchant fleet should be much larger than ours.

ARMY

Finally, Figure 10.5 shows the relative trends in Army personnel. I wanted to plot tank, artillery, and mortar trends, but could not find sufficient data.

(text continued on page 120)

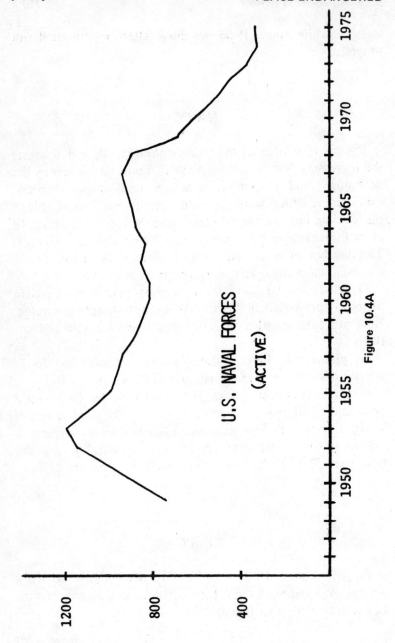

U.S. NAVAL FORCES
(ACTIVE)

Figure 10.4A

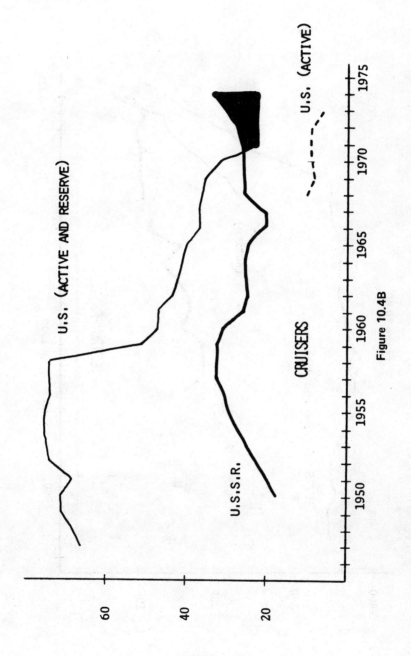

Figure 10.4B

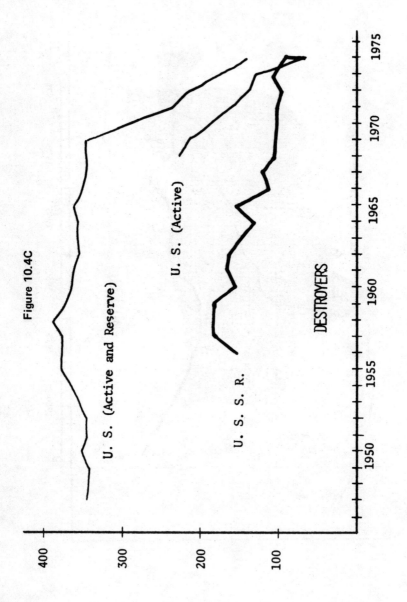

Figure 10.4C

DESTROYERS

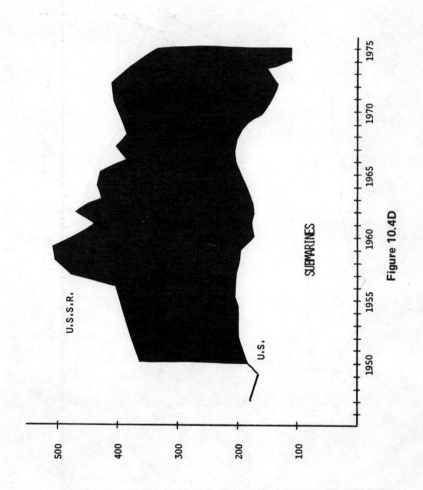

U.S.S.R.

U.S.

SUBMARINES

Figure 10.4D

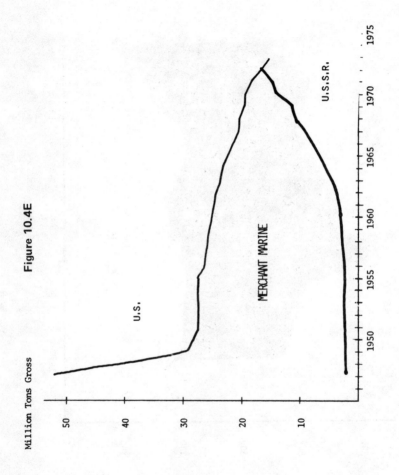

Figure 10.4E

Million Tons Gross

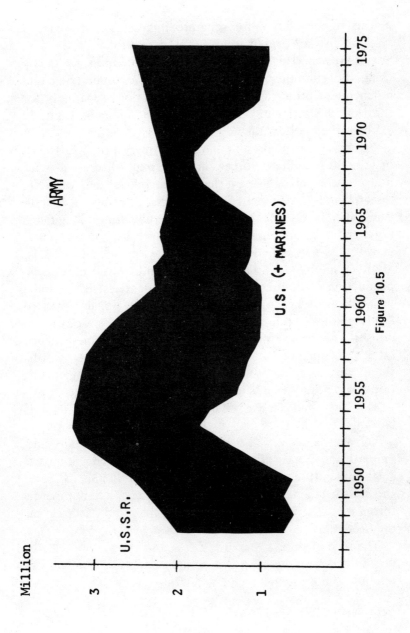

Figure 10.5

PRINCIPAL AMERICAN MILITARY TRENDS

The trends shown for separate indicators and weapons systems give an overall impression of American decline and Soviet growth. This impression can be made more precise by using the computer to define the distinct underlying and independent principal trends, which was done separately for the United States and the Soviet Union.[3] Appendix C briefly explains the methodology.

Figures 10.6A-C present the five primary principal trends in American military forces, military expenditures, defense budget as a percentage of the federal budget and of GNP, research-and-development expenditures, strategic expenditures, ICBMs, SLBMs, ballistic-missile submarines, long-range bombers, medium-range bombers, warheads, nuclear tests, megatonnage, yield, EMT, Air Force personnel, IRBMs, MRBMs, interceptors, tactical aircraft, military air transports, production of bombers, production of fighter/strike aircraft, production of helicopters, naval personnel, dollar worth of fighting ships, naval forces, carriers, submarines, destroyers, cruisers, merchant marine, Army personnel, reconnaissance satellites launched, and space launchings. In other words, these thirty-six trends reflect five underlying independent, principal military trends in American military power.

The first and largest is shown in Figure 10.6A and is labeled T_1. (The 0 on the vertical axis is the average for the principal trend over the thirty years, while the plus and minus 1 and 2 measure trend deviations of 1 and 2 standard deviations.) It defines the development of ICBMs, SLBMs, and missile submarines and their sharp increase in number in the mid-1960s. However, since 1968 this trend has been on the decrease.

The second principal trend, T_2, is also shown, and clearly delimits the decline of the American defense effort and its relation to both the Korean and Vietnam wars.

(text continued on page 124)

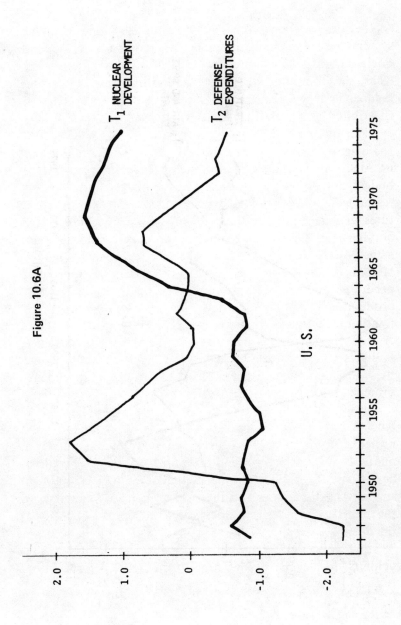

Figure 10.6A

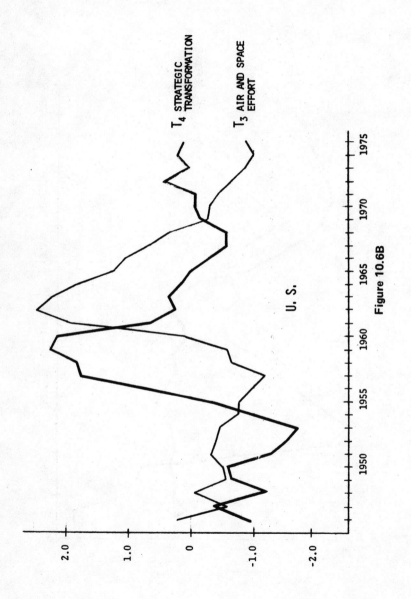

Figure 10.6B

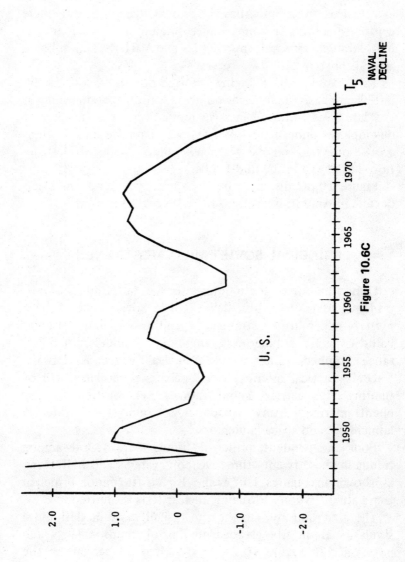

Figure 10.6C

Figure 10.6B plots the third and fourth principal trends. T_3 delineates the growth and decline in our air and space effort. This trend underlies the annual changes in our interceptor squadrons, reconnaissance satellite and space launchings, strategic expenditures, IRBMs and MRBMs, and military air transports.

T_4 measures our changing strategic doctrines, such as the initial emphasis on nuclear-bomb megatonnage and yield in the late 1950s under "massive retaliation," the subsequent de-emphasis under "flexible response," and the shift to numerous low-yield missile warheads under "assured destruction," or MAD, in the mid-1960s.

Figure 10.6C displays the final principal trend, the steep decline in American naval power.[4] It speaks for itself.

PRINCIPAL SOVIET MILITARY TRENDS

Using the same methodology as for the United States, principal trends were also delineated in Soviet armed forces, military expenditures, strategic expenditures, ICBMs, SLBMs, ballistic-missile submarines, long-range bombers, medium-range bombers, nuclear tests, nuclear warheads, IRBMs, MRBMs, tactical aircraft, naval personnel, dollar worth of fighting ships, carriers, submarines, cruisers, destroyers, merchant marine, Army personnel, reconnaissance satellite launchings, and space launchings.[5]

Four independent principal trends were found among trends in these twenty-three weapon systems and indicators, as shown in Figures 10.7A and B. A fifth minor principal trend almost wholly involving nuclear tests is omitted.

The first and by far the most significant in defining a similarity among the greatest number of trends is T_1, which is revealed in Figure 10.7A. It describes 38 percent of the variation in all the military trends, and particularly reflects

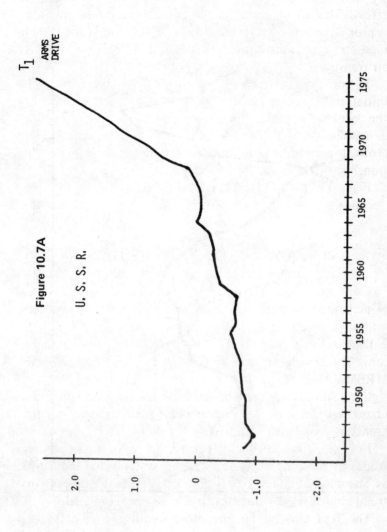

Figure 10.7A

U. S. S. R.

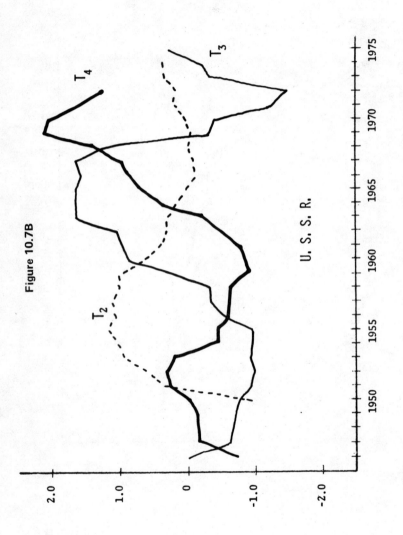

Figure 10.7B

Soviet growth in SLBMs, nuclear warheads, space launchings, ballistic-missile submarines, carriers, tactical aircraft, and military expenditures. T_1 clearly uncovers and projects the overall Soviet drive for military superiority. There is no trend like this for the United States, which disproves the claim that the Soviets are only responding to our initiatives. Also note that the trend has been accelerated since détente began in 1969, while all trends for the United States have been going down.

Figure 10.7B plots the three remaining minor principal trends. T_2 mainly delineates overall Soviet naval growth,[6] and underlies changes in her naval personnel, cruisers, submarines, military forces, and medium bombers. It shows that growing Soviet naval superiority is not so much a function of a rapid Soviet buildup as it is of American decline (compare with the American principal naval trend in Figure 10.6C).

The third principal trend, T_3, underlies worth of fighting ships, strategic expenditures, long-range bombers, MRBMs, destroyers, and IRBMs. The final principal trend largely defines trends in merchant marine and satellite launchings.[7]

Such are the principal trends in American and Soviet forces. The Soviets have one dominant and increasing upward military trend. The United States has no continuous upward trend, but a series of surges and declines.

PRINCIPAL TRENDS IN THE MILITARY BALANCE

What is most important is the changing balance. It is the *relative trends* that will matter—militarily and politically—in the future. In order to measure these relative trends, I calculated the annual quantitative difference in Soviet and American military forces, military expenditures, strategic expenditures, ICBMs, SLBMs, ballistic-missile submarines, long-range bombers, medium-range bombers, warheads, nuclear tests, IRBMs, MRBMs, tactical aircraft, naval personnel, dollar worth of ships, carriers, submarines, cruisers, destroyers, merchant marine, Army personnel, reconnaissance satellite launchings, and space launchings.[8]

When these twenty-three relative trends were then run through a computer, four clear and underlying principal trends were uncovered. They are shown in Figures 10.8A-D. In other words, the twenty-three Soviet and American military trends reflect four separate, underlying changing military balances.

The figures are organized so that the 0 line represents the average trend, and the plus and minus 1 and 2 measure 1 and 2 standard deviations from the average, calculated over the thirty years. Parity (the line of zero difference) is also shown on each figure. Any trend moving above the parity line defines American superiority; below the line defines Soviet superiority. Moreover, each figure shows the military trends of which it is a weighted sum.

Looking now at Figure 10.8A, the first principal trend, T_1, delineates the shifting balances in naval personnel, strategic expenditures, IRBMs, and SLBMs, as well as—to a lesser extent—tactical aircraft, satellite launchings, medium bombers, Army personnel, military personnel, and MRBMs. The parity line corresponds to the thirty-year average in this case, around which the balance favored America only during our arms increases resulting from the Korean and Vietnam wars.

The correlation between the military trends and T_1 are also shown. These correlations squared measure the proportion of variation of each military trend that manifests T_1 and the approximate weight each trend has in determining T_1. For example, T_1 underlies 86 percent ($.93^2$ x 100) of the variation in naval personnel. A plus or negative sign on a correlation indicates that T_1 is positively or negatively correlated with the military trend *over the years for which data on the trend were available.*

(text continued on page 133)

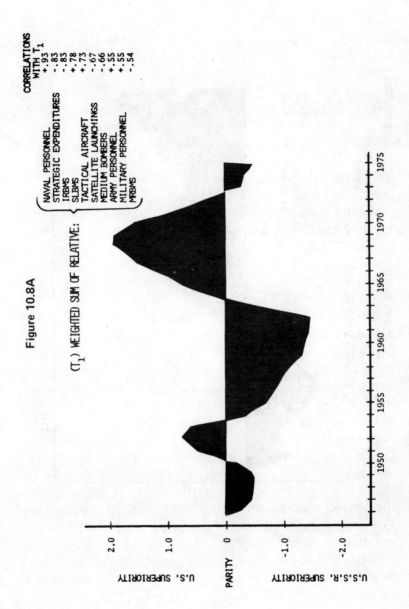

Figure 10.8A

(T_1) WEIGHTED SUM OF RELATIVE:

NAVAL PERSONNEL
STRATEGIC EXPENDITURES
IRBMS
SLBMS
TACTICAL AIRCRAFT
SATELLITE LAUNCHINGS
MEDIUM BOMBERS
ARMY PERSONNEL
MILITARY PERSONNEL
MRBMS

CORRELATIONS
WITH T_1
+.93
-.83
-.83
+.78
+.73
-.67
-.66
+.55
+.55
-.54

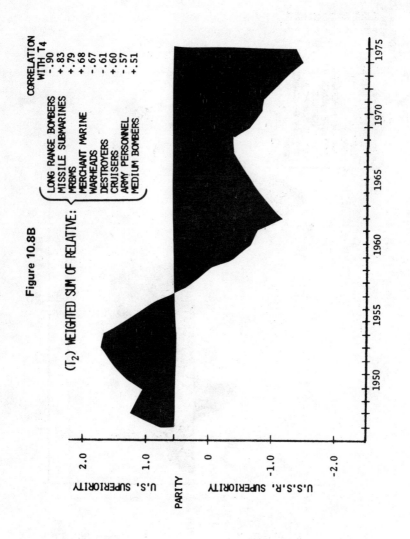

Figure 10.8B

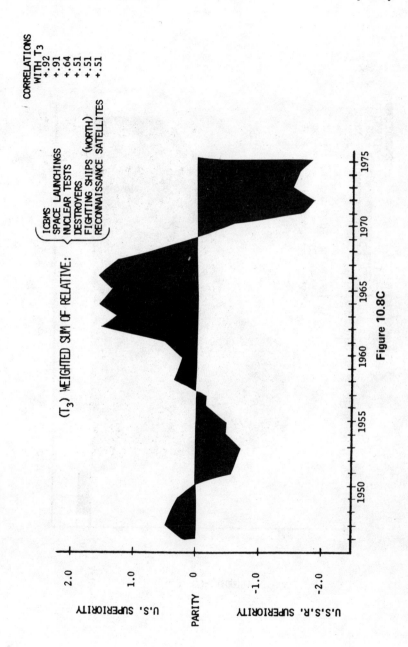

Figure 10.8C

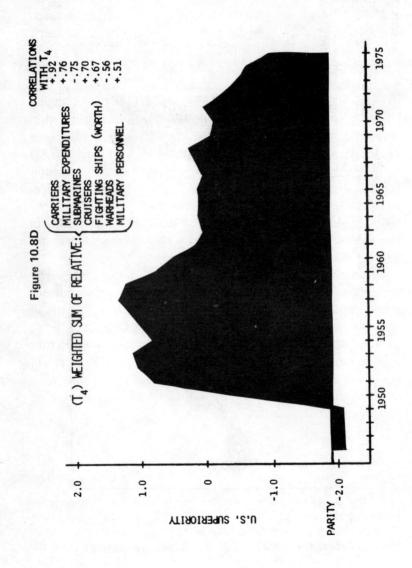

Figure 10.8D

(T_4) WEIGHTED SUM OF RELATIVE:

CARRIERS
MILITARY EXPENDITURES
SUBMARINES
CRUISERS
FIGHTING SHIPS (WORTH)
WARHEADS
MILITARY PERSONNEL

CORRELATIONS WITH T_4
+.92
+.76
-.75
+.70
+.67
-.56
+.51

U.S. SUPERIORITY

PARITY

Considering now the second principal trend shown in Figure 10.8B, T_2 shows a continual American decline from a peak during the Korean War. It underlies the changing balances in long-range bombers, ballistic-missile submarines, MRBMs, merchant marine, warheads, destroyers, cruisers, Army personnel, and medium bombers. Both T_1 and T_2 are the largest principal trends, underlying about 50 percent of the variation in all the military trends.

Figure 10.8C shows T_3, which underlies the changing balances in ICBMs, space launchings, nuclear tests, destroyers, dollar worth of fighting ships, and reconnaissance satellites. The final principal trend given in Figure 10.8D defines the changing balances in carriers, military expenditures, submarines, cruisers, dollar worth of fighting ships, warheads, military forces, and submarines.

It should be noted that the first three principal trends in the balance *now favors the Soviets, and all four trends are moving toward greater Soviet superiority.*

In sum, the computer analyses unveil an overall Soviet dominance—a potentially greater dominance given current trends—and a sharply accelerating upward Soviet trend. In virtually all cases, the American trend lines point down.

When this and Chapter 8 are put together, *the stark picture that emerges is of an overall Soviet superiority that will continue to grow. Moreover, this superiority is due to a concomitant Soviet drive for military dominance and an American retreat from arms.*

NOTES

1. The Soviet data for 1975 are based on recent testimony of Defense Secretary Rumsfeld before Congress and those for 1965 through 1974 are from former Defense Secretary Schlesinger's *Annual Defense Report FY 1976*, p. I-6; the 1952-1965 data are from the

International Strategic Institute's *The Military Balance, 1973-1974* and *1974-1975.* Part of the jump from 1974 to 1975, therefore, may be due to a difference in underlying definitions and sources.

2. The figures for the Soviet Union grossly underestimate Soviet expenditures, at least in the years from 1965 through 1975. Recent Soviet military expenditures are at least 42 percent greater than ours, but I could find no recomputation of past Soviet expenditures taking these new estimates into account. However, I have shown the new estimate for 1975 in Figure 10.1B.

3. The data presented in the preceding sections and in Chapter 8 were continuously updated and revised until this book went to press in April, 1976. However, the computer analyses were based on data I had as of October, 1975. Thus, in some cases the computer analyses were of data which for recent years differ slightly from those shown. In no way, however, should these data differences alter the conclusions.

4. The score for 1946 was omitted due to missing data in the underlying trend.

5. See footnote 3.

6. The scores for 1946-1949 and 1975 are omitted due to missing data in the underlying trends.

7. The scores for 1973-1975 are omitted due to missing data in the underlying trends.

8. See footnote 3.

The Soviet Drive Toward a First Strike

11

> One way to grasp our relative capabilities is to note that by
> 1977 the Soviets could, theoretically, initiate a counterforce
> strike against the U.S., absorb a U.S. counterforce response,
> and then still have sufficient forces to attack Chinese and
> NATO nuclear capability, attack U.S. population and military
> targets; and then still have a remaining throwweight larger than
> ours. Beyond 1977, things will get worse.
>
> —Malcolm R. Currie, Defense
> Department Director of Defense
> Research and Engineering,
> *Denver Post,* March 31, 1976

When all the arms data and trends have been considered,
the fundamental question remains. Does the Soviet Union
now possess, or will it soon possess, an ability to destroy our
offensive strategic forces and escape retaliation? If the answer
is yes, then swift military victory over the United States will
lie in Soviet hands.

An answer requires extreme care. We must work through a
thicket of technical considerations, the essential information

is secret and manipulated, and there are two sides to the question—one political and the other technical. The technical side concerns whether it is now, or would be in the future, physically possible for the Soviets to attack our strategic forces and destroy our retaliatory capability. That is, do—or will—they have a *preclusive first-strike* capability? The political side concerns the Soviet ability to significantly destroy our strategic offensive forces while deterring us from retaliating with what is left—that is, a *dominant first-strike capability*.

The differences between the two kinds of first strikes should be clear. The preclusive first strike is a matter of relative forces and their objective characteristics, warhead yield, accuracy, hardening of silos, anti-ballistic-missile protection, and so on. It is a matter of probabilities, reliabilities, and a mathematical model putting all the variables and parameters together. The existence of a preclusive first strike thus becomes a physical problem subject to technical solution.

A dominant first strike is also a question of weapons characteristics, probabilities, and equations, but it is not wholly subject to technical analysis because man's psychology, perceptions, and values are also at issue. It is partly a question of what constitutes a sufficient military threat to deter American leaders from retaliation and to invoke surrender. How we answer this depends on our political wisdom.

The weapons requirements for a preclusive strike are not the same as for a dominant first strike, and thus the basic reason for the distinction. The Soviets might not have, or be able to have, a preclusive first strike while being quite capable of obtaining a dominant one. The scenario presented in Chapter 1 of a Middle East war leading to a *dominant* first strike illustrates what the nature of this capability might be. Since a preclusive first strike requires more offensive and defensive strategic capability, its existence would assume a dominant one as well.

With these considerations in mind, I will take the more demanding case first. Does the Soviet Union now, or will it soon, have a preclusive first-strike capability? A full answer demands a technical discussion and elaboration of the factors involved, which include the characteristics of the Soviet and American offensive weapons (ICBMs, SLBMs, bombers), hardening of American missile silos, strategic defenses on both sides, missile reliability, number of warheads and yield, missile accuracy, defensive radars, and so on.

The technical discussion of all these factors is given in Appendix A. *The conclusion is that the Soviets will soon have a preclusive first strike, if not by 1977, at least by 1981.* This alarming conclusion assumes that the Soviets will not be deterred by and will absorb a counterblow that is likely to kill about 4 percent of their population, a number that is predicated on assumptions favorable to the United States. Thus, at a cost in lives half that of World War II and much less than that of imposing communism on the Soviet people, Soviet leaders could attack America and win.

What would they win? The almost universal belief is that an all-out attack on our ICBMs and bombers would kill tens of millions of Americans and obliterate our industrial capacity. This confuses an attack on our cities with one on our strategic forces.

An attack on our cities would kill some 100 million Americans immediately and from fallout.[1] However, our ICBMs are removed from urban areas, as are most of our forty-six SAC air bases. (There are exceptions, such as Whiteman Air Force Base, which is located near St. Louis.) Clearly, an attack on our forces should result in much fewer casualties. What would they be?

In testimony before the Subcommittee on Arms Control,

International Law, and Organization of the Senate's Committee on Foreign Relations, former Defense Secretary
Schlesinger provided data on the estimated impact of an
attack on our forces.[2] If each of our 1,054 ICBMs were hit
with two warheads, each of our SAC and missile-submarine
support bases with one, and all were detonated at optimum
height to maximize the lethal radius, and the month was
March (worst winds for fallout), from these "2,158 warheads" we would suffer 6.7 million killed and 5.1 million
injured. This assumes maximum use of civil-defense facilities.
Almost 99 percent of our manufacturing capacity would
survive, and the effects on our agriculture and livestock
would be negligible.[3]

*In other words, the United States would survive such an
attack as a viable society.* Our cities would remain largely
intact, as would our industrial might. America would still be
a handsome prize.

*A preclusive first strike is thus profitable, and possible in
the near future.*

This conclusion is based on a pyramid of assumptions
about reliabilities, probabilities, Soviet weapons and accuracies, and appropriate equations. They could well err on the
side of underestimating Soviet offensive and defensive strategic capabilities, since we are dealing with top-secret weapons. Moreover, even in such a framework of assumptions,
the Soviets are predicted to have a preclusive first-strike
capability soon. Clearly to me, at least, given the need for
one very large margin of error in which American survival,
and ultimately liberty, are at stake, prudence demands that
we act *as if* the Soviets soon will have a preclusive first strike.

However, to make an even stronger case for the danger we
face, I will turn the above argument around. Suppose that
because of the number of assumptions involved in the analyses in Appendix A and the possibility that I have overesti-

mated Soviet and underestimated American capabilities, the U.S.S.R. is unlikely to have a preclusive first strike in the foreseeable future. This has been the official American position. Moreover, it can be argued that, because of the enormous risk of taking action on the basis of assumption added on assumption, even if the Soviets felt they had a preclusive first strike they could not trust their equations sufficiently to take action. Even a small risk in the nuclear age is a deterrent, in Kissinger's view.

I will therefore assume, contrary to my results, that the Soviets will not have a preclusive first strike—that we will be able to retaliate effectively. In this case would the Soviets have a dominant first strike?

In the world of politics, the game is won not by objective capabilities alone, but by the bargaining equations in which capability plays a role along with interests and will. These equations invoke the whole matrix of subjective factors which we call the political process—the balancing of power. The question of a dominant first strike is whether, in spite of an objective capability to devastate Soviet cities, we would do so.

Consider again a Soviet surprise attack on American ICBMs and SAC bases. Let us presume the United States has a sufficient retaliatory force surviving to kill, say, 25 percent of the Soviet population, which is within McNamara's level of "assured destruction." Let us also presume that the Soviets possess in reserve thousands of warheads (of which she is clearly capable) and several hundred bombers able to hit the United States and at least fly on to neutral territory. Moreover, let us presume the Soviet attack is accompanied by threats that if we retaliate on her cities she will immediately unleash a full attack on our cities (remember, we have no ABM or significant fighter protection); that if we attack Soviet military installations, such as bomber bases, she will take out Chicago and New York; and that if we even try to attack one or two cities in a tit-for-tat manner, she will unhesitatingly retaliate on every major U.S. city.

No matter what we do, the Soviets would have *escalation dominance.* Because of our weaker strategic and conventional forces, whatever we try the U.S.S.R. could come back stronger (if we tried something with NATO, she could over-run Europe). Having been struck first, we also would have few remaining missiles and bombers for counterthreats or for an attack on her reserve missiles or bombers. Even if we knew the location of her reserves and tried to destroy them, our counterforce attack would be ineffectual, since the accuracy and yield of our warheads have been kept low so as not to constitute a provocative, and thus destabilizing, first-strike capability. And anyway, she could launch on radar warning of our attack.

In the words of Paul H. Nitze, Chairman of the Advisory Council, Johns Hopkins School of Advanced International Studies, former member of the SALT delegation, and former Deputy Secretary of Defense:

> By 1977, after a Soviet-initiated counterforce strike against the United States to which the United States responded with a counterforce strike, the Soviet Union would have remaining forces sufficient to destroy Chinese and European NATO nuclear capability, attack U.S. population and conventional military targets, and still have a remaining force throw-weight in excess of that of the United States. And after 1977 the Soviet advantage after the assumed attack mounts rapidly.[4]

Under these circumstances—and arguments for flexible response notwithstanding—surrender is the only option. This option would be reinforced if the Soviets shrewdly make it a question not of unconditional surrender, but one of our "leaving our hands off," say, the Middle East, and dismantling our remaining strategic forces. Although America would keep its national integrity and apparent sovereignty for a while, the eventual consequence would be the same: a totalitarian world.

Would our president then order a retaliatory blow in response to the attack and threat? Would he destroy Soviet cities, and thereby bear the responsibility for the annihilation of some 90 million additional Americans and most of our industrial capacity? Our weapons were meant to deter aggression. *If deterrence fails, would a president still press the button?* Of course not.

Our former Secretary of Defense, whose concern was maintaining the credibility of deterrence, was shockingly candid on this score in his *Annual Defense Department Report FY 1976 and FY 197T.* Recall that MAD rests on the premise that each side would retaliate on the other's cities if attacked and that this presumption supposedly provides a stable deterrence. Now along came James Schlesinger to say:

> For better or for worse, the scientist in the lecture hall who announces that, in response to a Soviet attack on our nuclear forces, we should destroy a hundred Soviet cities and their populations, *is unlikely to implement that threat should the situation arise.* [5]

> . . . the reaction of the policymaker in the face of such an attack cannot be foretold. But he and his advisors will have been exposed to a number of paper wars—i.e., hypothetical cases in which deterrence has collapsed and our opponent has launched some kind of a nuclear attack. They will know from these exercises that in many circumstances *the most suicidal course for the United States—and hence the least credible course—would be to strike the population of the opponent's cities.* . . .

> While the exercises may be hypothetical, the problem is not. The Soviet Union, for example, *now deploys a strategic nuclear capability that goes far beyond anything required by the theories of minimum or finite deterrence.* Her peripheral attack forces are

such as to be able to take under attack every significant target in Western Europe. Her central strategic systems are sufficiently large in numbers so that she could strike at a substantial number of military targets in the United States, and elsewhere in the world, *and still withhold a very large force whose future use we would have to consider in responding.*[6]

Thus did Schlesinger bury MAD, although its skeleton still props up détente. And thus did he also bury his idea of flexible targeting. For with such a reserve coupled with escalation dominance, a Soviet threat to hit our cities if we retaliate simply must be believed, *after they have already attacked us.*

The Soviets will have this dominant first strike soon, if they do not already. And the analysis given here in conjunction with the data and computer analyses of the relative military balance and trends shown in the preceding chapters are sufficient to assume that *the Soviets will have a preclusive first strike,* soon.

The accomplishment of a first strike explains the astounding Soviet drive toward military and especially strategic superiority. The desire for a first strike and the final defeat of capitalism explains why the Soviets do not follow the action-reaction theory—as we have been engaging in unilateral disarmament, they have continued their massive buildup. The drive for a first strike explains why they have not been restrained by détente, as Kissinger would have it, and have never become as "sophisticated" in the abstract theory of MAD.

NOTES

1. "Briefing on Counterforce Attacks," September 11, 1974; made public on January 10, 1975.
2. Ibid.

3. Ibid., pp. 49-50.

4. "Assuring Strategic Stability," *Foreign Affairs,* Vol. 54 (January, 1976), p. 226.

5. James R. Schlesinger, *Annual Defense Department Report FY 1976 and FY 197T* February 5, 1975, p. II-1, italics added.

6. Ibid., p. II-2, italics added.

War
or Surrender

At one time there was no comparison between the strength of the USSR and yours. Then it became equal to yours. Now, as all recognize, it is becoming superior to yours. Perhaps the ratio is just greater than unity, but soon it will be 2 to 1. Then 3 to 1. Finally it will be 5 to 1. I'm not a specialist either, I suppose, but this can hardly be accidental. I think that if the armaments they had before were enough, they would not have driven things further. There must be some reason for it. With such a nuclear superiority it will be possible to block the use of your weapons, and on some unlucky morning they will declare: "Attention. We are marching our troops to Europe, and if you make a move, we will annihilate you." And this ratio of 3 to 1, or 5 to 1, will have its effect: you will not make a move.

—Aleksandr Solzhenitsyn, Speech
before the AFL-CIO, New York
National Review, August 29, 1975

When Aleksandr Solzhenitsyn, the symbol of man's irrepressible struggle for liberty against tyranny, came to the United States in June, 1975, President Ford was advised by Henry Kissinger not to see him because such a meeting would indicate the President's sympathy for this passionate and moral humanist, and of course would affront Soviet leaders. Détente, and thereby peace, would be endangered.

Senator Jesse A. Helms in a Senate speech well characterized this consequence of détente:

> I suggest that this is a sad day for our country if the United States of America must tremble in cowering timidity for fear of offending Communists unless the President of the United States refuses to see a dedicated exponent of freedom—a dedicated Christian, I might add—a Nobel Prize winner, who comes to our country as a visitor.[1]

Some light was shed on Kissinger's incomprehensible advice by Warren Rustand, appointments secretary to President Ford, who claimed that this snub of Solzhenitsyn was the result of a Soviet-American agreement entered into at the time of his exile,[2] an agreement that we would not exploit his freedom in the West against the U.S.S.R.

Whatever the reason, Kissinger's incredible advice throws into sharp relief the difference between this man and Solzhenitsyn, and between two contrary foreign policies for dealing with the Soviets.

As presented in Chapter 3, the Kissinger policy combines two elements for achieving a single purpose—avoiding a nuclear war.

The first element is academic theory, a belief that peace is enhanced by embedding adversaries within a net of mutually beneficial cooperative agreements, exchanges, and activities. Thus, trade, cultural, scientific, and political arrangements with the Soviet Union are to be pursued vigorously on the theory that her leaders will be less inclined toward confrontation if they risk severing very advantageous agreements.

The second element involves maintaining our strength with regard to the Soviet Union and meeting whatever challenges or aggression they present. The role of power is not to be ignored, but American power is to be used only *defensively*. It is to be minimized to avoid an arms race and to avoid antagonizing or threatening the Soviets.

Peace through cooperation, through just sufficient defensive power. This is the meaning of détente.

By contrast, Solzhenitsyn's goal is to expose a totalitarianism whose leaders give lip service to détente while continuing the Cold War to overcome Western strength and resolve. He argues that the peace bought by détente is illusory. He does not urge an American attempt to overthrow communism—a forward, as opposed to a defensive, policy; he simply asserts that we should stop giving aid and comfort to Soviet leaders by providing them with the means both to control their slave-state and to defeat Western freedoms.

For Solzhenitsyn, the fear is communist hell. For Kissinger the overwhelming fear is nuclear war, and he sees his policy as the only means to prevent this. Ironically, *it is Kissinger's formula that is putting us in the position of having to choose between nuclear war and communism.* It is Solzhenitsyn who provides the way out.

Consider the elements of détente. Regarding the first element, will transactions and collaboration promote peace? It is astounding how this theory, the favorite of many cloistered academics, should become the official American policy concerning those who are dedicated to overthrowing Western politico-economic systems. On this academic theory I have shown in Chapters 4 and 5 that:

—there is no historical basis for it;

—there is no scholarly-scientific demonstration of it;

—there is no consistent, quantitative-empirical evidence for it.

Regarding American power, as I have shown in earlier chapters, under détente we have:

—been decisively surpassed by the Soviet Union in conventional military power;

—given them a dominant first-strike potentiality;

—risked the strong possibility of their achieving a preclusive first-strike capability against American strategic forces.

In sum, the Nixon-Kissinger-Ford defensive interpretation of American power has put the United States in the position of being militarily, and thus politically, one down.

But even with the erosion of American defensive power and the lack of proof that detente will work, many believe that peace is worth the gamble. The major argument against Solzhenitsyn, and for détente, is that we must not risk nuclear war. Before discussing this belief let me first deal with Solzhenitsyn's case.

He argues that we are aiding Soviet leaders to overcome the West and spread communism. Consider that under détente:

—we have extended considerable economic aid to the Soviets (how many Americans realize this?) and are providing them with whole factories, with food, and with technical scientific aid in their space and satellite programs, among others;

—Soviet leaders have vigorously pursued their defeat-the-West, Cold War strategy (consider Vietnam, Portugal, the Middle East, and Angola), but now through détente;

—the Soviets have followed an aggressive military-armaments program whose object could only be the defeat of the West;

—the Soviet people continue to be fed all the Cold War lies and distortions about the West.

Solzhenitsyn is correct. *The Soviets are being aided and abetted by their potential victims.* Soviet leaders have given every indication of continuing the Cold War behind a détente facade, of conducting a political war while preparing for a hot one.

Many recognize this, but conclude that détente is our only alternative to war. This is wrong.

Throughout history, peace has been maintained by clear purposes, military power, and the will to use it. Peace is preserved when potential aggressors know that the rewards are not worth the costs of war. *When a nation's purposes become confused, its strength eroded, or its credibility questioned, aggression against it is encouraged, and is likely to occur.*

Détente and its management have communicated serious weakness. The Soviets have been encouraged to pursue an ambitious program of armament and subversion of the West that was not possible during the Cold War. The risk of war is now greater than ever before. Moreover, and this is where Solzhenitsyn is also correct, détente is putting the United States in a position of strategic surrender to the Soviets. Americans may have no choice but to bow to nuclear blackmail. Soon.

For American and the West détente is increasing both the risk of war and of defeat. We will have only the choice between war or surrender. For this legacy détente may be most remembered.

NOTES

1. *The New York Times,* July 17, 1975.
2. Associated Press, August 12, 1975.

A New Realism

13

*This will remain the land of the free only so long as it is the
home of the brave.*

—Elmer Davis
But We Were Born Free

Not détente, but a new realism is required. A policy of
realism recognizes that interaction among different cultures
and antagonistic ideologies is a process of building structures
of expectations among them. These structures are momentary balances of interests, capabilities, and will (or credibilities); they are temporary status quos defining spheres of
influence, rights, and obligations. If these structures become

incongruent with what people or nations want and can and will do, they become increasingly unstable, susceptible to sudden disruption by some final straw. Conflict is then the means through which a new structure of expectations—a cooperative framework—is worked out. *Conflict and coopera-tion go together.* Both must be kept in mind to understand order and interactions among nations. They are the two faces of man.

A policy of realism, therefore, first enables cooperation to flow from a balance with underlying interests, capabilities, and will. Too much cooperation, as well as too little, can upset relations among nations. *Cooperation must evolve from what nations want and can and will do.* Pushing nations to cooperate beyond their desires, means, or will can disrupt the framework of their relations and cause severe conflict. Not harmony but violence is produced by rationally constructing artificial cooperative structures between antagonists. Idealists the world over have yet to learn this basic fact of social man.

Second, a policy of realism recognizes that some conflict now is better than a more severe one later. Conflict reorders expectations that are out of balance with what people and nations want, can get, and will exert themselves for. If fear of conflict rigidifies the status quo, then such structures will become more and more removed from reality until there is an explosion of violence. Low-level conflict produces positive change. It is not to be feared, but accommodated (as mar-riage counselors have discovered recently). The proper culti-vation of low-level tension and conflict can ease nations (as it can families) through trying transition periods and eventually promote a harmony that might otherwise be only that of the dead or vanquished.

Finally, a policy of realism assumes that conflict and violence are not caused by lack of cooperation, person-to-person contact, or interaction. Indeed, violence occurs at all levels of social intimacy and international relations. Nor is conflict a result of a rich-poor gap, cultural propensities, or capitalism. Rather, conflict is a product of the process of social interaction itself, and it is bound up with the balance between man's desires, abilities, and determination. *Conflict is a political phenomenon, a manifestation of disequilibrium in this balance.* Ultimately, conflict arises when some person, some group, some nation decides that who gets what from whom, or does what, and when, is unjust in terms of their power, and must and will be changed.

A policy of realism recognizes that a cure for violence lies not in objective but in subjective conditions. It lies in attending to the balance of interests, of capabilities, of will. It lies in allowing lower-order conflict to change this balance before a severe incongruence between the framework of order and its supporting balance can cause violence. The cure lies in politics.

Regarding now the Soviet Union, a policy of realism knows that the bedrock American national interest is the support of liberty, wherever it exists, wherever it is threatened. The rights to freedom of speech, of religion, and of the individual to pursue his own life and happiness—the essence of America—have made this a land of unequaled opportunity, affluence, and liberty. In this interdependent world, when the freedom of one is diminished, that of free men everywhere is threatened. The liberty of Americans will not be preserved as an island in a sea of totalitarianism.

The primary struggle between the United States and the Soviet Union is not a struggle of geopolitical interest, resources, or spheres of influence. Nor is it a competition between "systems." It is a moral struggle. It is between whether man will determine his own life or have it forcefully determined for him by some self-selected elite, and whether inalienable rights protect man from becoming the total subject of the state.

The struggle between the Soviet Union and the United States is a protracted conflict in which the central and long-run goal of Soviet leaders is to defeat Western freedoms and bring the world under totalitarian influence and control. Short-run Soviet agreements and negotiations are always a part of this single long-run objective.

What, then, is a policy of realism vis à vis the Soviet Union? The following six principles should guide such a policy.

First, we must lose no opportunity to contrast American freedoms with the totalitarianism under which Soviet citizens are forced to live. We should reaffirm our fundamental support of freedom and recognize our identity of interests with free men everywhere. We should understand that a strong national interest can be based only on *moral ideals,* and that America has the ideal of freedom woven into its national fabric.

Second, Americans must be informed about the truth of our military inferiority, and about Soviet aims and military power. Americans will respond with courage and resolution if they recognize that freedom is under an attack from which it may not survive and that America's military might has deteriorated. A resurgence of the American spirit is possible. But people must be enlightened at every opportunity about what it is that endangers us—life under communism, the terror and repression used to maintain a totalitarian system, the tens of millions of Soviet lives snuffed out. Then American dedication to protect freedom against this absolute tyranny can be reborn.

Third, we must rebuild our conventional military capability to meet communist threats wherever they occur, whatever their nature. This would raise the threshold for using nuclear weapons and reduce the risk of an escalation to nuclear war.

Fourth, we must improve the invulnerability of our offensive strategic forces and more than match the Soviet strategic drive. The probability of nuclear peace depends on an American superiority. Moreover, we must appreciate that deterrence can still fail, and that therefore, through active and passive strategic defense, we must protect our cities against blackmail and attack.

Fifth, we must stop aiding the Soviet Union. The investment in military superiority by the Soviet leaders is eased by American and Western aid and trade. Moreover, the ability of Soviet leaders to maintain their control over their people is enhanced by Western technology and products. *If communism is truly superior, let it show this without help from its self-proclaimed capitalist enemies.*

Finally, we must continue to negotiate with the Soviet Union on issues and mutual problems, such as scientific and environmental questions and arms-control possibilities, but accept, in good old Yankee bargaining fashion, only terms that are to our immediate and practical benefit. We should avoid agreements that enable the Soviets to harvest short-run gains by giving lip service to long-run abstractions like peace, cooperation, and relaxation of tensions.

In sum, a new realism would understand that communism is our proclaimed enemy. A policy of realism would comprehend that freedom with dignity and peace can be bought only by asserting our national interest in freedom, by informing Americans about the threat we face, by rebuilding our military power. Thomas Paine's remark in the year of our nation's birth still applies today:

> Those who expect to reap the blessings of freedom must, like men, undergo the fatigue of supporting it.

Appendices

Appendices

A Soviet Preclusive First Strike

The United States maintains a strategic force composed of three systems: ICBMs, strategic bombers, and Polaris and Poseidon nuclear submarines. Nuclear deterrence rests on the ability of any one of these systems to survive an attack. I will consider each in turn, beginning with our land-based ICBMs.

THE INVULNERABILITY OF AMERICAN ICBMS

A number of factors are involved in the ability of our ICBMs to survive a surprise attack, which include the number, accuracy, and yield of the warheads attacking them; the protection given to our ICBMs; electronic interference (fratricide) effects; and so on. Kosta Tsipis, a senior researcher at the Stockholm International Peace Research Institute, has assessed the interrelationship among a number of these factors to determine the survivability of our ICBM force.[1] He tends to underestimate the capability of the Soviet missile force and therefore will provide a conservative first approximation of her first-strike ability.

According to Tsipis, we have 1,054 ICBMs—54 Titans, each with over a 5-megaton warhead; 450 Minuteman II missiles, each with a 1-megaton warhead; and 550 Minuteman III missiles, each with three 160-kiloton MIRV warheads. The Minuteman III ICBMs are housed underground in silos hardened to withstand an overpressure of 1,000 pounds per square inch (psi); the rest are in silos of 300 psi. Is this ICBM force invulnerable?

According to Tsipis, the U.S.S.R. has for a sudden attack the following ICBMs: 209 SS-7, 8 of them with 5-megaton warheads; 288 of the heavy SS-9, each with a 20-megaton warhead; 970 SS-11, each with a megaton warhead. There are also the submarine-launched missiles (SLBM), of which there are 528 SS-N-6 with 1-megaton warheads and 80 SS-N-8, each with a 1-megaton warhead. These data are for 1974 and are considerably below the current size and power of Soviet missiles. By the end of 1975 four new types of missiles were operational, including the SS-18, which is a larger successor to the SS-9, and capable of carrying a 50-megaton warhead or 8 MIRVs; the SS-17, which can carry four 2-megaton MIRV warheads; and the SS-19, which can carry five 2-megaton MIRV warheads. Nonetheless, let us see where Tsipis' optimistic data lead him.

He first determined a coefficient called K that measures how lethal a warhead must be to destroy a missile in a silo with a specific probability and which is a function of a warhead's accuracy and yield.[2] If there are S number of silos, then KS measures the overall lethality of opposing warheads required to destroy S silos. If there are N number of warheads, then KN measures the overall lethality of the warheads. When KS = KN, the number of warheads is just sufficient to destroy the number of silos.

Tsipis tabulated the number of warheads, yields, and accuracies of American and Soviet ICBMs and SLBMs and their KS and KN, taking into account silo hardness. Table A-1 summarizes his relevant data. As can be seen, the Soviets seem to have nowhere near the ability to destroy a high percentage of American missile silos as of 1974. Even if we were to focus on the Soviets' 288 SS-9s, the most powerful of their missiles then and the one provoking first-strike fears in the hearts of analysts, and it is assumed that 50 percent of its warheads will fall within one nautical mile (CEP = 1) of the silo, these SS-9s could destroy only 45 of the 504 silos

Table A-1

Total lethality (KS) required to destroy all U.S. or U.S.S.R. silos with probability (p) of .97 and .90 and the total lethality (KN) available to the U.S.S.R. and the U.S. (all 1974 data)

Total KS Required*

	p = .97	p = .90	KN Available	
for U.S.	82,080	54,170	3,864	to U.S.S.R.
for U.S.S.R.	40,000	26,300	18,648	to U.S.

*Assuming silos are hardened as follows.

U.S.: 550 silos at 1000 psi; the remainder at 300 psi.

U.S.S.R.: 1,100 silos at 100 psi; 400 at 300 psi.

hardened to withstand 300 psi, or 19 of those 550 hardened to 1,000 psi. And all this is assuming 100 percent availability and launch reliability of the missiles and overlooking the interference effect (fratricide) of nearby nuclear explosions.

In sum, this optimistic analysis shows a very large gap between 1974 Soviet capabilities and what is required for a first strike. However, this assumes a very poor accuracy of their missiles, an accuracy which may be underestimated by as much as a factor of 2 or more. For example, some[3] have estimated the powerful SS-9 to be almost twice as accurate as Tsipis assumes. Such a change in estimate can enlarge Tsipis' K coefficient for this missile from 7 to 29, *or by more than four times the silo-killing capacity that he gives it.* If the accuracy is four times that which Tsipis assumes, his lethality K explodes form 7 to 116—a multiple of over 16 times. That this higher accuracy is not unlikely, consider the following information supplied Congress by the Department of Defense: "We have some information that the Soviets have achieved, or will soon achieve, accuracies of 500-700 meters with their ICBMs."[4]

This would be about a fourth to a third of a nautical mile, or accuracies four and three times that which Tsipis assumes. To show the effect of Soviet accuracy if it is four times as great as Tsipis estimates, the KN available to the Soviets in Table A-1 would change from 3,864 to 64,032, or an amount of power likely to destroy 90 percent of our ICBMs.

As a consequence, the KP values in Table A-1 are subject to sharp increase for the Soviets if in fact their accuracies approach anything like ·our own, which are estimated at a CEP of .5 for the Titan, .3 for the Minuteman II, and .2 for the Minuteman III.

But working within Tsipis' optimistic assumptions the answer is clear: the Soviets did not have a preclusive first-strike capability as of 1974.

Will they have one soon? In another analysis, Tsipis has extended his KN values for the Soviet Union into the future as "possible Russian responses" to announced U.S. progress.[5] We can take these values as representing the future Soviet kill *capability*.

Judging from Tsipis' plotted projections the Soviet Union will have (as a worst-case estimate—that is, the top of a range of possible capabilities) KNs of about 80,000 in 1980, 200,000 in 1981, and 800,000 in 1985.[6] According to Table A-1, a KN of 54,170 could destroy about 90 percent of our silos; a KN of 82,080 could destroy about 97 percent. Thus, by 1981, the Soviets would have a possible 200,000 KN to a needed 82,080 KS. This disparity should compensate for the possible unreliability of some of their missiles and the fratricide effects on warheads aimed at the same or close targets. Moreover, we must remember that this may be based on an estimate of Soviet warhead accuracy that is off by a factor of 2, which would quadruple the KN of 200,000, or even a factor of 4, which would raise the KN to over 3 million!

Tsipis does not indicate what Soviet responses he is plotting. I do not know whether he has taken into account their new, MIRVed, and more accurate missiles now made operational (such as the SS-17, SS-18, and SS-19). The SS-18 and SS-19 have been estimated to have a CEP of .25,[7] which, if true, according to his way of calculating the lethality of a missile, K, would give the Soviets an assured ability to obliterate our land-based missiles by 1980. In any case, even his optimistic assumptions lead to the pessimistic conclusion that by at least 1981 the Soviets could destroy all but less than a dozen of our ICBMs (99 percent effective).

What happens if our assumptions are pessimistic to begin with? Phyllis Schlafly and Chester Ward have presented data and analyses bearing on this question in their book *Kissinger on the Couch*.[8] They argue that around 1977 the Soviet Union will be able to destroy our ICBMs. They assume their missile accuracy (CEP) will be 1,000 feet and that the Soviets can launch 300 SS-9, 100 SS-18, and 20 SS-17 or SS-19 ICBMs with a total of 2,634 warheads (mainly two megatons apiece) totaling two equal waves. The second wave could be launched at the same targets after a delay of six minutes. The number and power of these warheads should destroy all but six of our ICBMs (even if 150 ICBMs were protected by 100 ABMs at Grand Forks, North Dakota, which will no longer be the case). Moreover, before their warheads impact, 30 Y-class submarines could explode SLBM warheads over our silos at the moment we receive the warning of a Soviet ICBM attack to pin down through interference effects our ICBMs until the Soviet ICBM warheads arrive.

Another way of looking at the survivability of our ICBMs is in terms of the total throw-weight available to the Soviet Union, as does Paul Nitze.[9] Within the limits of the Vladivostok accord, *10 to 12 million pounds of throw-weight* "can be expected" to be available to the Soviets. Compare this to a *net throw-weight of only about 4 million pounds necessary to threaten the destruction of 92 percent of our ICBMs.* This assumes silos hardened to 1,000 psi, a CEP of .125 nautical mile, two warheads targeted on a silo, and taking reliability into account. Clearly, the Soviet Union will have enough throw-weight to destroy all but a handful of our ICBMs, and have enough left over to threaten our cities and deal with our allies.[10]

In other words, in considering the data of Tsipis, Schlafly and Ward, and Nitze, *pessimistic assumptions lead to a possible destruction of our ICBMs by 1977; the optimistic assumptions postpone this possibility only for a few years.*

THE RETALIATORY CAPABILITY OF AMERICAN STRATEGIC BOMBERS

But the destruction of our ICBMs is only part of a preclusive first-strike equation. What about our long-range bombers? We can assume that the Soviets will attack without warning and even though 30 percent of our bombers may be on fifteen-minute alert, most would still be caught on the ground. Our SAC bases can be attacked with fractional orbital (FOB) missiles which would give no more than three minutes' warning to the bombers. This means that the SAC bases would be hit more than fifteen minutes before our ICBMs (an ICBM warhead from the Soviet Union would take about thirty minutes from launch to impact), but pin-down nuclear explosions could be set off above our ICBM fields by FOBs and SLBMs to prevent launching of our Minuteman before the Soviet ICBMs arrive. Only 92 to 138 warheads with relatively low accuracy would be needed to destroy our forty-six SAC bases.

At the most optimistic, 20 percent of our bombers may survive.[11] In 1975, we had 437 long-range B-52s. If we also optimistically assume that 300 are available and reliably on line in the 1977-1980 period, then about 60 might survive. On their flight toward the Soviet Union and attempts to penetrate to target, these bombers would face a swarm of 2,700 interceptors, many new and including the latest and fastest MiG-25 Foxbat, and 9,500 surface-to-air (SAM) launchers (not counting reloads). About half these SAMs are SA-2s with a slant range of 25 miles, and a number have more than double this range. Moreover, the Soviets have about 5,000 defensive radars to guide their planes and SAMs to our 60 bombers. Finally, our bombers will try to penetrate at very low altitude and may confront a Soviet AWACS/fighter air-defense system with a look-down, shoot-down capability. We have demonstrated that such a system is possible.[12]

Taking all this into consideration, where there is an average of 45 interceptors and hundreds of SAMs to attack each bomber (remember, the Soviets planned the surprise attack and will be ready for our bombers), it would be remarkable if any survive. However, again to be optimistic, assume 20 percent make it to target or are able to fire standoff air-to-surface (ASM) missiles (with 1-megaton warheads). Of these 12 bombers surviving, assume four would be of the old B-52 D type and perhaps carry four 1- to 5-megaton bombs and one ASM; the remainder would be of the G-H type and possibly carry in addition to these bombs 12 to 20 200-kiloton SRAMs (short-range attack missile) and two ASMs apiece.

In total, therefore, we could expect to arrive on target an optimistic 48 bombs totaling 48 to 240 megatons, 20 ASM of 20 total megatons, and 96 to 160 SRAMs of 19.2 to 32 total megatons. If the megatonnages per weapon are converted to equivalent megatons (EMT) through the formula EMT = $NY^{2/3}$, where N equals the number of warheads (or bombs) and Y their yield, then we get a total EMT for this surviving bomber force of 101 to 215 EMT. This measures the total optimistic retaliatory power of our surviving long-range bomber force. A problem is evaluating the significance of this power, a point I will return to after considering our submarine force.

THE RETALIATORY CAPABILITY OF
THE AMERICAN SUBMARINE FORCE

Many feel that none of our bombers and few of our ICBMs could survive a nuclear attack, but that our invulnerable submarines constitute the heart of our deterrent. In considering the deterrent effect of our Polaris and Poseidon and future Trident missiles, we must consider the number of submarines on station, the number vulnerable to anti-submarine warfare (ASW), the number of warheads and yield, and the possible anti-ballistic missile (ABM) defenses of Soviet cities. This is quite an order.

The best study of all the factors involved in an effective submarine deterrent that I know of is by Geoffrey Kemp.[13]

He developed several models interrelating various assumptions about these factors, such as the number of surviving submarines and the strength of the Soviet ABM defenses. To use his results let us first establish three damage levels which might range up to what the Soviets might consider unacceptable. These are presented in Table A-2, and are based on those by Kemp.[14]

Now a basic question concerns the pounds per square inch (psi) overpressure needed to achieve these damage levels. Kemp assumes 5 psi is sufficient.[15] However, civil defense has been a serious concern in the Soviet Union. For over a decade urban populations have been prepared for a possible nuclear attack; shelters and evacuation plans have been arranged. And they have even boasted that their civil defense will limit the number of deaths from a total U.S. attack on their cities to around 6 percent of their population.[16] Since we are talking about a retaliatory attack on Soviet cities, surely the people will be ready. For these reasons, we must consider a least a partial implementaion of an all-out civil-defense effort.

Table A-2
DAMAGE LEVELS

Damage Level	No. of Largest Cities Hit	Immediate Fatalities[a]	% of Population[b]	% of Industrial Capacity at Risk
L-1	10	10.5	4.3	25
L-2	50	23	9.4	50
L-3	200	37	15.0	62

a. This does not include fatalities from delayed fallout effects.

b. Total population assumed to be 244.7 million.

The problem is then what overpressure to use to determine damage levels L-1 to L-3, considering civil defense. To severely damage a reinforced-concrete building above ground, a psi of 11 to 15 is required; underground shelters, available to half the urban population, can protect people from overpressures of 25 psi.

Treating 5 and 25 psi as lower and upper bounds, I will take 15 psi as the appropriate overpressure from which to compute the number of warheads of given yield to cause a specific level of damage.

Kemp provides a table[17] of the number of warheads required to cover an area with 5, 10, and 20 psi. On the average, the warheads required for 10 and 20 psi are about 2.5 and 5.7 times those necessary for 5 psi. I will therefore estimate that Kemp's results should be multiplied by 4 to bring them up to a psi of about 15—that is, to compensate for a partially prepared and protected Soviet urban population.

Applying this conversion value of 4, we can then use Kemp's results to assess the retaliatory damage our missile submarines could inflict on the Soviet Union. The results of converting Kemp's results for Poseidon submarines are shown in Table A-3 and categorized as to how many would be necessary to penetrate Soviet defenses under various assumptions and cause the stated level of damage. Around 1980, the American strategic nuclear submarine fleet should consist of 31 Poseidon, 7 Polaris (A-3), and 3 Trident submarines. The first Trident should enter the force in mid-1979, and thereafter two may be produced per year to replace the Polaris until there are 11 Trident and 30 Poseidon in all.

To be sure the table is clear, for the first column with the specified conditions as a limited ASW Soviet ability and 100 ABMs in the Moscow area with a single-shot kill probability of $P = .8$, 24 Poseidons would be required (with a total EMT of 521) for a damage level of L-1; for a damage level of L-2,

44 Poseidons (with a total EMT of 956) would be needed. The number required takes into account that only half will be on station and an overall reliability of .8 for the SLBM.

This table gives us a basic matrix for determining the American retaliatory capability under different Soviet strategic defense levels. It is obvious that in most cases our poten-

Table A-3
TOTAL POSEIDON SUBMARINES (OR EMT) REQUIRED IN FLEET UNDER SPECIFIED CONDITIONS[a]

| | Limited ASW | | | | Improved ASW | | | |
| | ABM^c | | ABM^c | | Upgraded ABM For Major Cities | | Upgraded ABM For All Areas | |
Damage Level[b]	P=.8	P=.4	P=.8	P=.4	P=.8	P=.4	P=.8	P=.4
L-1	24* (521)	20* (434)	32* (695)	28* (608)	56 (1216)	28* (608)	176 (3823)	108 (2346)
L-2	44* (956)	40* (869)	64 (1390)	60 (1303)	96 (2085)	72 (1564)	252 (5473)	136 (2954)
L-3	76 (1651)	72 (1564)	88 (1911)	88 (1911)	124 (2693)	104 (2259)	320 (6950)	184 (3996)

a. The figures in parentheses are the EMT equivalent to the number of Poseidons shown, where EMT is calculated taking yield to the two-thirds power. The number of Poseidons is computed assuming half are on station, the overall reliability of SLBMs is .8, 16 SLBMs per submarine, and 10 x 50 kiloton MIRVs per SLBM.

b. P = a single shot probability.

b. Defined in Table A-2.

c. ABM defense of Moscow area and consisting of 100 missiles.

*Falls within U.S. planned submarine capability for 1980, which should be 31 Poseidon, 3 Trident, and 7 Polaris (A-3) submarines, with a total EMT of 850-1159, depending on whether one assumes 10 MIRVs or 14 MIRVs per Poseidon and Trident SLBMs. It is assumed that the Polaris (A-3) will have six 40 kiloton MIRVs for each of sixteen SLBMs; that the Poseidon will have sixteen SLBMs and 50 kiloton MIRVs; and that the Trident will have twenty-four SLBMs and 50 kiloton MIRVs.

tial fleet would be inadequate to retaliate at any of these levels. If the Soviets are given an unrealistically limited ASW and only 100 ABMs around Moscow, we could reach an L-1 damage level; if we had 14 MIRVs per Poseidon and Trident SLBM, we could just reach the L-2 level.

However, if they improve only their ASW, we could no longer reach L-2, but L-1 is possible. Even if the ABMs were upgraded to cover other major cities but had only a P = .4, we could still reach L-1. In all other cases, even L-1 is improbable.

Table A-3 is an optimistic assessment from a U.S. deterrent and retaliatory point of view. The reliability of .8 for our SLBMs is much higher than we have been able to achieve so far. Moreover, for those warheads that penetrate Soviet defenses, it is assumed that they are evenly spread out over an urban area to maximize damage. Duplicate hits or urban misses are not considered. This is an especially important assumption in consideration of the requirement for a large number of 50-kiloton warheads to blanket a sprawling urban area. For example, in order to produce a 5 psi overpressure over all of Moscow (and thus cause 50 percent fatalities for those unprotected) 43 evenly distributed, 50-kiloton warheads are required.[18]

Considering Soviet ABM capability, which columns in Table A-3 are most realistic? More than likely, the Soviets will have an extensive ABM system awaiting our missiles. They have not only the Galosh system around Moscow but also the Tallinn system of radars and SAMs. They have over 1,000 SA-5 SAMs with high ABM capability and a 100-mile range, and thousands of SA-2 which also have an ABM capability, a 30-mile slant range, and 100,000-foot altitude. They have a mobile SAM, the sophisticated SA-6, which has an ABM possibility. Moreover, their Henhouse long-range radars are up to a half a mile long and 100 feet high and can track warheads at thousands of miles. They also have a

Doghouse network with ranges of over a thousand miles, and numerous other radars that can be hooked into an ABM net. Thus, the rightmost columns in Table A-3 are probably most realistic, but as can be seen it would require an American missile submarine fleet much larger than is planned for even an L-1 damage level.

TOTAL RETALIATORY CAPABILITY

Now, let me put all this together for our three strategic offensive systems in terms of some criteria of an effective (i.e., deterring) retaliatory capability. For McNamara this was the ability to destroy one-fifth to one-fourth of the Soviet population and one-half to two-thirds of her industrial capacity.[19] L-3 in Table A-2 comes closest to this criteria (but is still less than what McNamara considers necessary). I will therefore consider L-3 the damage required for deterrence.

Now we have the essential technical data and the criteria for what constitutes effective deterrence. Do the Soviets have a preclusive first strike?

First, in the early 1980s with their improved missile systems they are likely to be able to eliminate virtually all of our ICBMs with a sudden strike.

Second, they would be able to destroy most of our bombers, but those left which—we will optimistically assume— could penetrate massive Soviet defenses would still carry a tremendous power, which was calculated at an EMT of 101 to 215. Based on the calculations of Geoffrey Kemp on the 50-kiloton warheads required for given damage levels at 5 psi,[20] we can determine the EMT necessary (remembering to multiply by 4 to convert to 15 psi), where yield is taken to the two-thirds power. For damage levels L-1 to L-3, these are 123, 303, and 523 respectively (considering that a 50-kiloton warhead has an EMT of .14).[21]

Thus, a surviving EMT of 101 to 215 does reach a damage level of L-1, barely, or a capability of killing around 4.3 percent of the population and putting at risk 25 percent of the industrial capacity (also assuming evenly distributed warheads or bombs).

Finally, there may still be some American ICBMs to launch, although probably less than a dozen. Assume that there are four Minuteman II, each with a 2-megaton warhead; and six Minuteman III left, each with three MIRVs of 200 (instead of the more likely 170) kiltons. Regardless of the Soviet radar and ABM or SAMs converted to ABM, also assume that all these warheads will make it through to target. Their total EMT would be 25. This added to the 101 to 215 for surviving bombers does not change the picture. An L-1 damage level is the best that can be achieved.

In total, then, a Soviet first strike in 1980 would risk, at most, about a 4.3 percent of her population and 25 percent of her industrial capacity from surviving ICBMs and bombers. Our submarines alone—and making the most optimistic assumptions about reliability, distribution of warheads, and so on—might achieve the same level. But considering their ABM potential, this L-1 is unlikely.

Table A-4 combines all the above calculations and conclusions. When the retaliatory power of all the remaining ICBMs, bombers, and submarines is considered, an L-1 level of destruction is probable, and an L-2 level is possible, but unlikely. There is no way these calculations would enable us, realistically, to reach L-3.

In sum, our total retaliation would probably kill about 4 percent of the Soviet population, or 10 million people. This is half the cost of World War II to Soviet leaders, and about one-sixth the minimum estimate of 25 million Soviet citizens who have died from communist terror and repression.

Recall that McNamara's lower limit of assured destruction was 20 percent of the population (49 million people) *or*

Table A-4

U.S. RETALIATORY CAPABILITY
AFTER A SOVIET FIRST-STRIKE

Damage Levels[a]	Required EMT[b]	Retaliatory Capability in EMT		Probable SLBM damage[e]	Total Probable Damage ICBM + SAC + SLBM
		ICBM[c]	SAC[d]		
Less than L-1		25		high probability	low probability
L-1	123		101-215	low probability	high probability
L-2	303			very improbable	low probability
L-3	523			impossible	impossible

a. See Table A-2.
b. Assuming 15 psi overpressure required for 50 percent fatalities.
c. Assuming 4 Minuteman II and 8 Minuteman III survive and all warheads make it to target.
d. Assuming 60 SAC bombers survive and 4 B-52 D and 8 B-52 G-H types penetrate to target.
e. See Table A-3.

about twelve times as much as the most probable number our retaliatory force would kill, and even five times more than an improbable level of 10 million people killed (L-2).

The conclusion is inescapable. After a surprise attack, we could not effectively retaliate. Our ability to deter a Soviet first strike is rapidly deteriorating. *And around 1980, and perhaps as early as 1977, the Soviets will have a preclusive first strike.*

NOTES

1. "Physics and Calculus of Countercity and Counterforce Nuclear Attacks," *Science,* Vol. 187 (February 7, 1975), pp. 393-397.

2. K = two-thirds power of Y divided by CEP squared, where Y is the yield of a warhead and the CEP is its accuracy in nautical miles.

3. Harry Gelber, *Nuclear Weapons and Chinese Policy,* Adelphi Papers No. 99 (London: International Institute for Strategic Studies, 1973).

4. "Briefing on Counterforce Attacks," by James R. Schlesinger before the Subcommittee on Arms Control, International Law, and Organization of the Senate Committee of Foreign Relations, September 11, 1974, p. 10.

5. "The Accuracy of Strategic Missiles," *Scientific American,* Vol. 233, (July, 1975), pp. 14-23.

6. Ibid., p. 23.

7. William R. Van Cleave, "Soviet Doctrine and Strategy: A Developing American View," paper presented at the conference on The Future Role of Soviet Military Power Within the East-West Political Context, Institute of the Stiftung Wissenschaft und Politik, Ebenhausen, May 1-2, 1975.

8. New Rochelle: Arlington House, 1975, pp. 64 ff. and *passim.*

9. "Assuring Strategic Stability," *Foreign Affairs,* Vol. 54 (January, 1976) p. 230, footnote 19.

10. The next issue (February, 1976) of *Foreign Affairs* contained an article by Jan M. Lodal ("Assuring Strategic Stability: An Alternative View") critical of Nitze's conclusions about the future destructive capability of Soviet ICBMs. Lodal claims that if "by 1985 the Soviets were able to increase this yield to 1.5 megatons and improve accuracy to 0.15 nautical miles, this could increase the probability of destroying a silo with two warheads to about 85 percent."

Lodal gives no formula for these calculations, but they appear overly optimistic. According to the *Strategic Survey* (1969, p. 32), the accuracy and yield assumed by Lodal would lead to a 99 percent probability of destroying a 300 psi silo with *one* warhead. Using formula 12b given by Tsipis ("Physics and Calculus . . .," op cit, p. 396) and employing Lodal's assumptions as to yield, number of warheads, and accuracy, I arrive at a 98 percent probability of destroying a silo hardened to 1,000 psi. These results favor Nitze rather than Lodal.

11. Edward Luttwak, *The Strategic Balance 1972* (New York: The Library Press, 1972), pp. 32-34.

12. James R. Schlesinger, *Annual Defense Department Report FY 1976 and FY 197T,* February 5, 1975, p. II-34.

13. *Nuclear Forces for Medium Powers; Part I: Targets and Weapons Systems* and *Parts II and III: Strategic Requirements and Options,* Adelphi Papers 106 and 107 (London: The International Institute for Strategic Studies, London, 1974).

14. Ibid., Parts II and III, p. 5. Per his assumption, I am taking 50 percent of his population at risk as fatalities.

15. Ibid., Parts II and III, p. 5.

16. Donald G. Brennan, "When SALT Hit the Fan," *National Review,* July 23, 1972.

17. Kemp, op. cit., Part I, p. 18.

18. Ibid., Part II-III, p. 24.

19. Robert S. McNamara, *The Essence of Security* (New York: Harper & Row, 1968), p. 76; and Statement of Secretary of Defense Robert S. McNamara before a Joint Session of the Senate Armed Services Committee on Department of Defense Appropriations on the Fiscal Year 1968-72 Defense Program and 1968 Budget, January 23, 1967, p. 39.

20. Kemp, op. cit., Parts II and III, Table 2. Based on the warhead assumed for the Poseidon. This is a convervative assumption. If the Poseidon carries 14 MIRVs per SLBM, each warhead may be as small as 17 kt.

21. These EMT for damage levels L-1 to L-3 should not be confused with the EMT given in Table A-3, which are for the total fleet and not the on-target EMT.

Military
Data Sources

The military data for the years 1946-1975, analyzed in Chapters 8 and 10, were aggregated from a variety of sources.

Among the most helpful for comparative data was *The Military Balance* published annually by the London International Institute of Strategic Studies; the *Yearbook of World Armaments and Disarmament* of the Stockholm International Peace Research Institute; the annual reports to Congress of the Secretary of Defense and the annual reports to Congress on the military balance by the Chairman of the Joint Chiefs of Staff.

The publications of the private American Security Council of Washington, D.C., had much useful data, especially *The Changing Strategic Military Balance U.S.A. vs. U.S.S.R.* (1967), *The ABM and the Changed Strategic Military Balance U.S.A. vs. U.S.S.R.* (1969). Moreover, the monthly *The Defense Monitor* of the private Washington, D.C., Center for Defense Information provided useful information.

The National Strategy Information Center published some helpful sources, especially Norman Polmar, *Soviet Naval Power* (Strategy Paper No. 13, 1972) and *The Military Unbalance* (Strategy Paper No. 9, 1971).

A surprising amount of military data was also available in the annual *Aerospace Facts and Figures.* In addition, comparative naval data were available in the annual *Jane's Fighting Ships,* of course.

Some specific studies that had especially useful data were John M. Collins and John Steven Chwat, *The United States/ Soviet Military Balance: A Frame of Reference for Congress* (Congressional Research Service, The Library of Congress, January 21, 1976); Edward Luttwak, *The Strategic Balance* (The Center for Strategic and International Studies, Georgetown University, 1972); J. I. Coffey, *Strategic Power and National Security* (University of Pittsburgh Press, 1971), *World Military Expenditures and Arms Trade 1963-1973* (ACDA, n.d.); *Strategic Survey 1969* (IISS, London, 1970); Edgar M. Bottome, *The Balance of Terror* (Beacon Press, 1971); Alton H. Quanbeck and Barry M. Blechman, *Strategic Forces* (A Brookings Institution Staff Paper, 1973); George Quester, *Nuclear Diplomacy* (Dunellen Co., 1970); Phyllis Schlafly and Chester Ward, *Kissinger on the Couch* (Arlington House, 1975).

A great deal of military data were also found in various articles in the *Bulletin of the Atomic Scientist, Scientific American, Washington Report,* and *Strategic Review.*

Many other sources were consulted and were helpful for individual datum.

Methodology

The quantitative technique used to determine the principal trends for Chapter 10 was component time series analysis.

The matrix of military data was organized so that the variables defined the separate weapons systems or indicators (ICBMs, cruisers, etc.); and the cases, or rows of the matrix, were the years 1946-1975. An additional time variable (1946, 1947 . . . 1975) was added to the matrix, as well as a dichotomous measure of those years the United States was at war.

The full matrix was 84 variables by 30 years and had an average of 14 percent missing data.

These data were intercorrelated using a pair-wise deletion, missing data correlation program (SPSS). The principal axes of this correlation matrix were then determined, and those axes (components) with eigenvalues greater or equal to unity were rotated to an orthogonal varimax solution. Factor scores were computed for each of the rotated components.

These factor scores are the principal time trends shown in Figures 6-8 of Chapter 10.

By virtue of this methodology, each principal trend:

—represents a clustering of military trends with similar profiles;

—is the "center of gravity" of the cluster (within the constraint that the principal trends are mutually orthogonal);

—is statistically independent of the other principal trends;

—shows the most likely future direction of movement in the cluster of trends.

For a technical discussion of the overall methodology, see my *Applied Factor Analysis* (Evanston: Northwestern University Press), especially the sections on the component model, principal axes, and P-factor analysis.

Glossary

ABM: anti-ballistic missile

Assured Destruction: an unacceptable level of destruction the United States could cause the Soviet Union in response to a Soviet first-strike attack on the United States; this level was defined by Robert McNamara at between one-fifth to one-fourth of the Soviet population and one-half to two-thirds of the Soviet industrial capacity; see MAD

ASW: anti-submarine warfare

ballistic-missile submarines: submarines capable of firing SLBMs

bus: the part of a MIRVed missile's payload that carries the re-entry vehicles and has a guidance package, fuel, and thrust devices for altering the ballistic flight path so that the re-entry vehicles can be dispensed sequentially toward different targets

CD: civil defense

CEP: circular error probability, which is a measure of the delivery accuracy of a weapon system used as a factor in determining probable damage to targets; it is the radius of a circle around the target at which a missile is aimed within which the warhead has a .5 probability of falling; the radius is usually given in nautical miles

Counterforce Doctrine: the strategic doctrine which emphasizes attacking an opponent's military targets, and especially strategic capability

credibility: the believability of a nation's promises or threats

cruise missile: a guided missile which uses aerodynamic lift to offset gravity and propulsion to counteract drag; the major portion of a cruise missile's flight path remains within the earth's atmosphere; only long-range strategic cruise missiles are considered here

détente: the foreign policy aimed at minimizing the risk of nuclear war with the Soviet Union through cooperative transactions and arms control;
Détente I: one of two elements of détente, which emphasizes imbedding the Soviet Union in a web of transactions with the United States and will give her a stake in preserving them, thus reducing U.S.-Soviet conflict;
Détente II: the second element of détente, which emphasizes maintaining sufficient U.S. power to deter Soviet aggression while restraining an assumed conflict-generating arms race through arms control

deterrence: the state of deterring, by virtue of the costs or risks it would entail, another nation from action it would otherwise take;
nuclear deterrence: the state of deterring, by virtue of the nuclear retaliation it might incur, another nation from a first strike with strategic nuclear weapons

dominant first strike: see first strike

ECM: electronic countermeasures

EMT: a measure of the explosive yield of a nuclear warhead which adjusts for the waste of explosive energy of larger weapons by overconcentration at the center of the explosion; EMT is often calculated as the two-thirds power of the yield in megatons times the number of warheads with that yield

escalation-dominance: a nation has escalation-dominance over a second nation in a conflict when no matter what military choice the second makes, the first nation can top it

first strike (nuclear): initial strategic nuclear attack on an opponent before he has used any strategic weapons himself;

dominant first strike: a first strike backed up with a sufficient reserve of strategic nuclear weapons to deter the opponent from retaliating with any strategic nuclear weapons

preclusive first strike: a first strike of sufficient power to destroy the opponent's strategic nuclear retaliatory capability, or sufficient defensive strategic power to lower the damage from nuclear strategic retaliation to acceptable limits.

FOB: fractional orbital bombardment; an FOB missile achieves an orbital trajectory, but fires a set of retro-rockets before the completion of one revolution in order to slow down, re-enter the atmosphere, and release the warhead it carries into a normal ballistic trajectory toward its target; compared to an ICBM, an FOB missile substantially reduces the time between radar sighting and warhead impact

IRBM: intermediate-range ballistic missile, with a 1,500- to 4,000-mile range

K: the lethality of a nuclear warhead to a silo, which equals the yield of the warhead in megatons to two-thirds power, divided by the square of the CEP in nautical miles

kiloton: a measure of the yield of a nuclear weapon equivalent to 1,000 tons of TNT; the Hiroshima atomic bomb equaled 13 kilotons

megaton: a measure of the yield of a nuclear weapon equivalent to 1 million tons of TNT, i.e., 1,000 kilotons; all the bomb tonnage dropped on Japanese and German cities during World War II equals two megatons

MAD: Mutual Assured Destruction; a doctrine assuming that a stable nuclear environment obtains when neither the United States or the Soviet Union has a first-strike capability, and both have the capability to retaliate on the other if attacked and cause unacceptable damage; see assured destruction

MIRV: multiple independently targeted re-entry vehicles carried by an ICBM or SLBM

MRBM: medium-range ballistic missile, with a 500- to 1,500-mile range

MTE: see EMT

NATO: North Atlantic Treaty Organization

nuclear deterrence: see deterrence

nuclear retaliatory capability: the strategic offensive nuclear weapons surviving a first strike and available for retaliation

preclusive first strike: see first strike

psi: pounds per square inch

SAC: Strategic Air Command

SAM: surface-to-air missile; primarily used against aircraft, although some are convertible to ABM

SALT I: the 1972 agreements between the Soviet Union and the United States signed in Moscow on May 26, 1972, that resulted from the Strategic Arms Limitation Talks begun in Helsinki in 1969; the agreement consists of two accords, one of which limits the ABMs of both nations to two missile-defense systems each of no more than 100 launchers per system; the other accord consists of limitations on offensive strategic weapons

second strike: the offensive nuclear forces surviving a first strike for a retaliatory attack against the aggressor; sometimes this concept is used to refer to the nuclear forces an aggressor may keep in reserve after launching a first strike; see first strike

silo: the housing, usually made of concrete, for an ICBM that protects it against blast, heat, or radiation from a nuclear attack

SLBM: submarine-launched ballistic missile

SRBM: short-range ballistic missiles, with a range of less than 500 miles

SSBN: U.S. nuclear submarines which carry SLBMs

SSM: surface-to-surface missile

stable nuclear environment (strategic stability): encompasses both crisis stability and arms stability, and refers to a relationship in which neither side has an incentive to initiate the use of strategic nuclear forces in a crisis, or perceives the necessity to undertake major new arms programs to avoid being placed at a strategic disadvantage

strategic: relates to a nation's military, economic, and/or political power and its ability to control the course of military/political events;
strategic offensive nuclear weapons: nuclear-weapons systems designed to be employed against enemy targets in order to effect the destruction of the enemy's political/economic/military capacity;
strategic defensive nuclear weapons: nuclear-weapons systems designed to protect a nation against strategic offensive nuclear weapons

tactical nuclear weapons: nuclear weapons for use on the battlefield to affect the outcome of a battle

throw-weight: this is the maximum useful weight which has been flight-tested on the boost stages of the missile; useful weight includes weight of the re-entry vehicles, penetration aids, dispensing and release mechanisms, re-entry shrouds, covers, buses, and propulsion devices with their propellants (but not the final boost stages) which are present at the end of the boost phase

Vladivostok accord: an agreement reached in November, 1974, between President Ford and Soviet Communist Party leader Brezhnev which places a ceiling of 2,400 on the strategic missiles and bombers each side could have, and a limit of 1,323 missiles with MIRVs

warhead (force loading): that part of a missile, projectile, torpedo, or bomb that contains the explosive intended to inflict damage; only strategic warheads are considered here

yield: the force of a nuclear explosion expressed in terms of the number of tons of TNT that would have to be exploded to produce the same energy